BEASTS IN MY BED

Jacquie Durrell is married to Gerald Durrell—the Durrell of *The Overloaded Ark* and *The Bafut Beagles*—and Mrs Gerald Durrell is sick and tired of being told how lucky she is to have such a famous husband and lead such a glamorous life. Very much a personality in her own right, she decided to describe her own experiences of living with the Durrells and their animals.

So she wrote this book about her entry into the Durrell menagerie and her subsequent encounters with beasts both human and animal. Her astringent and very personal observations on the situations in which she found herself will appeal to anyone who has read her husband's books, visited the Jersey Wildlife Preservation Trust Zoo, which they started together, or seen their various successful television series on animal collecting in remote parts of the world. Those who read and relished Gerald Durrell's *My Family and Other Animals* can also renew their acquaintance with the rest of that intriguing and now famous family.

JACQUIE DURRELL

Beasts in My Bed

with footnotes by
GERALD DURRELL

Collins
FONTANA BOOKS

First published 1967
First issued in Fontana Books 1968
Seventh Impression August 1973

© Jacquie Durrell 1967

Printed in Great Britain
Collins Clear-Type Press
London and Glasgow

For
DURRELL
My Favourite Beast

The cover photograph by Jane Burton
is reproduced by permission
of Bruce Coleman

ILLUSTRATIONS

(between pp 96 and 97)

CHAPTER 1

I am tired of the endless stream of people who tell me how much they envy my 'glamorous life' and how lucky I am to have such a famous husband. 'What more,' they cry ecstatically, 'could any woman want out of life?' Well, frankly, it is far from glamorous and any husband, famous or not, still has to be lived with—unfortunately.

Although our meeting, and eventual elopement, were in the finest tradition of the leading women's magazines, there was certainly no air of romance about them. In fact, I once shocked somebody by telling him that I only married Durrell to get back £15 he owed me.[1]

Gerry Durrell's intrusion into my life was annoying and upsetting for everyone concerned. Being by nature a rather solitary person, and also scornful of people whom I considered to be shallow, spoilt and wholly extrovert,[2] I viewed Mr. Durrell at first with grave suspicion.

My poor demented father had been persuaded by a rather cunning friend of his to acquire a seedy commercial hotel as a 'profitable side-line'. I was appalled when I saw this gloomy hole, and even more appalled when I met the crowd of chattering females that infested it. These turned out to be refugees from the Sadler's Wells Opera Company, who were spending two weeks of their provincial tour in Manchester. I would normally have sympathised with them at having to suffer the Mancunian climate, but since they could do nothing but talk about some marvellous being who apparently had everything any woman could possibly desire, I lost patience with them.[3]

[1] This is a gross libel. G.D.
[2] I was, at that time, modest, unassuming and with a shyness that would have been envied by the average gazelle. G.D.
[3] You can see by virtue of the fact that this book was written in the first place, that she eventually came round to their way of thinking. G.D.

7

Then one wet Sunday afternoon the peace was shattered by a mass of female forms cascading through the living-room door and dragging in their wake a rather delicate-looking Rupert Brooke-ish young man. Judging by their idiotic behaviour, this could only be the Wonderboy himself—and it was. I examined this creature carefully and found myself rather amused by his posturings.[4] However, he suddenly realised I was looking at him and fixed me with a basilisk stare. I beat a hasty retreat and deserted the field.

During the following two weeks we happily saw very little of one another, until one morning when my harassed step-mother begged me to escort Mr. Durrell to the railway station as the poor unfortunate young man had no idea where it was—a thing I found very difficult to believe. Since all his female admirers had had to go to rehearsal, there was no one else available, but I made it quite clear that I was only doing it under protest.

Having finally satisfied himself that I was not overjoyed at having him as a companion, Mr. Durrell went out of his way to exert every facet of that great charm which was so much admired by females in general. When this did not produce any marked results he switched to humour and, much to my annoyance, he did amuse me—so much, in fact, that I was sorry to see him go.[5] I began to feel slightly guilty that I had not been exactly fair to him in the past, but as I would probably never see him again I did not let it worry me.

At last the large house was empty and my father felt that now he could set about renovating the place. Soon the entire establishment was seething with plumbers, plasterers, carpenters and decorators, and we, the family, were incarcerated in what rooms the workmen allowed us to use. In the middle of this organised chaos came Durrell. Could

---

[4] I have never postured in my life. The fact that a certain *je ne sais quoi* that I had acquired did not appeal to the earthy, peasant-like mentality of the author should not, I feel, be laid at my door. G.D.
[5] The rot starts to set in. G.D.

we accommodate him for a short time, while he visited
all the zoos in the area to get orders for his forthcoming
animal collecting expedition to British Guiana? My step-
mother, being a sympathetic soul (and not knowing any
better), agreed to have him, providing he was willing to
put up with all the noise and inconvenience and eat with
us as a family. That was all he wanted, and he was soon
well established, exchanging saucy badinage with my step-
mother and engaging my father in long, involved discussions
on current events.

He quickly became everybody's friend except mine.
Knowing how I felt about him, he nevertheless had the
temerity to ask my father's permission to take me out to
dinner, and, what was even more amazing, I found myself
agreeing. When I got used to the idea I was pleased. I was
between boy-friends and thought it might be amusing to
spend an evening with such a 'man of the world'. Much
to my astonishment, I thoroughly enjoyed myself and we
got on extremely well together.[6] He told me all about his
work as an animal collector, and I told him what it was
like studying to be an operatic singer. He then switched to
talking about his family, who sounded wildly fascinating
and quite different from my own background. My parents
had separated when I was two and I had been thrown
around from one person to another, living with either
grandparents or a weird collection of aunts and uncles.
Having no real family life of my own, I envied Gerry his
happy childhood and the security he had had, and because
of this I found myself telling him things that I had never
told anybody before. By the time we returned home, I had
lost any feelings of distrust or animosity I had had, and
really felt that I had at last found a friend whom I could
talk to and relax with.

This worried me a great deal, as I felt that I could very
easily get far too involved with someone like that—which

[6] Having had by this time fairly considerable experience in dealing
with wary animals, I kept somewhat inanely agreeing with everything she said. Hence we got on extremely well together. G.D.

was a bad idea since I had to devote every moment to
music. It was a relief to me that we did not keep in touch
with each other during the next six months while he was in
British Guiana, although we had both promised faithfully
that we would write. I was very busy gaining experience
in public singing, and was, in fact, far too occupied even
to think about what Gerry might be doing.

So it was a great shock to find him sitting in our living-
room one May afternoon, looking extremely fit and (even
to my rather jaundiced eye) attractive. He quickly explained
what he was doing in Manchester again. Having returned
to the United Kingdom with the bulk of the collection,
which was housed in the local zoo, the idea was that he
should dispose of the animals as quickly as possible and send
money out to his partner, who was still in Guiana, to enable
him to bring back more animals. Of course he persuaded
my step-mother once again to allow him to stay with us,
which was quite sensible as he was out at all hours of the
day and night cleaning, feeding and looking after his
charges, and to be treated as a guest would have made it
very awkward for everyone.

I was appalled at the idea of having this disturbing
influence around for so long, so I was even more determined
to be off-putting. Soon he counter-attacked by embarking
on a deliberate campaign to break down my opposition.
It began quite simply. Would I help him prepare a series
of animal lists for him to circulate around the various
zoos? They had to be typed, and as I had free access to
my father's machine he thought it would be better for me
to do them than for him to ask permission to use this
much valued piece of equipment. Thinking that this might
speed his departure and enable me to get on with my real
work, I embarked upon the gargantuan task. I never knew
there were so many different types of birds and animals in
the world. What on earth were Macaws and how could a
Squirrel Monkey be one and the same thing?—What was a
Giant Anteater, for heaven's sake? I bombarded Gerry with

endless queries and he patiently tried to explain things to me.

'Look, it's no good, you'll just have to come up to the zoo and see the animals for yourself,' he said.

This did not appeal to me at all, as I held very strong views on the ethics of keeping any wild creature in captivity, and in any case most of the zoos I had ever visited were horrible, smelly places where I would not dream of keeping a dead cat. Strangely enough, Gerry did not try to persuade me or pressure me into going with him the next day, neither did he defend zoos in general, but he did try to explain what the real function of a well run zoo should be, and how vital it was, in the face of the population explosion and the spread of civilisation, that wildlife should be preserved for future generations.

Zoos, he argued, would eventually be the last sanctuary for wild things as man increased in numbers and slowly encroached on the natural habitat. He told me how whole herds of wild game were being shot as part of a misguided tsetse fly campaign in Central Africa. Elsewhere, dams were being constructed and vast areas flooded that were the natural feeding grounds of many wild creatures. It was inevitable that when the interests of man conflicted with those of wild life, the animals would go to the wall. His most cherished ambition in life was to create a special zoo where he could keep and breed some of these creatures in the hope that they would not be completely exterminated, and the one thing he felt passionately about was that all zoos must cease to be mere show places and become true scientific institutions where the welfare of the animals was of paramount importance.

He talked like this the whole way to the zoo, and before I realised it we were inside a large wooden building which vibrated with the chatterings and squealings of animals. The first thing I noticed was the lack of smell that I normally associated with zoos. Instead, there was a pleasant odour of straw, food and warm animal bodies. Yet the thing that most impressed me was Gerry's relationship with all these creatures. Suddenly, this seemingly shallow young man became a different person. Gone was the diffident air as he walked solemnly up and down the lines of cages, giving each creature titbits and talking to them. He really cared about them, and they, in a funny way, returned this love[7] and interest with obvious trust. Like small children, they would scream out to attract his attention, or jump up and down eagerly, waiting to be noticed. I followed slowly behind him along the passageways and peered, I admit rather timidly, into each cage, becoming quite absorbed by these lovely creatures. The streamlined Giant Anteater, looking for all the world like a futuristic car, walking carefully up to the front of his compartment to be patted; the multi-coloured Macaws, shouting 'Robert' in different keys: the charming little Squirrel Monkeys sitting like clowns with their heads on one side. Without doubt, all these animals knew that they were being looked at in a special way, and yet they did not appear to resent my being there—I almost felt as if they had accepted me.

We spent quite a long time there, while Gerry gave every animal a second feed and renewed any wet straw, and I just sat on a box and watched him. He worked quietly and efficiently, obviously enjoying himself, and talking to every animal as he passed. He had certainly forgotten that I was there, and concentrated his entire attention on the animals. The whole thing fascinated me and it was with reluctance that I broke the silence to ask him questions about the various creatures.

'Well, at least I'll know what I'm writing about,' I said as we returned home, 'and I must say, they really are fascinating.'

After this visit to the zoo our friendship expanded. I was working at the time in my father's town office, where I received a flood of telephone calls. Would I have lunch

---

[7] She had yet to learn that animals generally return the love you lavish on them by a swift bite in passing—not unlike friends and wives. G.D.

with Gerry that day or, if not, what about morning coffee or afternoon tea? How about going to the theatre or was there a good film I wanted to see? My father enquired rather acidly who was paying my salary, as I seemed to spend most of my time away from his office.

'Don't worry, Dad,' I assured him, 'we're just good friends and he'll be going away soon, anyway.'

A grunt was the only reply I got, but he was quite obviously worried that I might be overwhelmed by all the attention I was receiving from a man who was so totally different from my usual male friends.

Much to my parents' relief, Mr. Durrell calmly announced one morning that he would be leaving us soon, as all the animals had gone and there was really no reason to keep him in the north; in any case he had not yet seen his mother, so he felt he ought to go back to Bournemouth. This time, I took him to the station a little more eagerly than before.

As I got back to the office the telephone was ringing. It was my father, enquiring whether Gerry had got away safely.

'Yes, he has,' I replied.

'Now perhaps we can all do a bit of work,' he said, and then followed a list of instructions. Replacing the receiver, I turned towards my desk. The office door burst open and framed Gerry Durrell clutching a large bouquet of faded chrysanthemums to his bosom. He thrust them towards me, saying rather obviously, 'These are for you.' Then he hesitated as he turned to leave: 'You wouldn't like to marry me, would you?'

He shrugged his shoulders and grinned wryly. 'I didn't think you would,' he said and left the office.

My father's relief was not long lived, for by every post I received either a letter or a postcard and, on a few occasions, long telegrams. Then came the awful day when a large parcel arrived for me; this was too much for my father. He summoned me to his private room.

'Now look here, Jacquie, there must be something between

you and that Durrell chap. No man wastes his time and his money on writing to a girl and sending her expensive presents if he doesn't expect something in return. Now I want the truth, however unpleasant.'[8]

Trying not to laugh at my normally rational parent's behaviour and attitude, I tried with absolutely no success to convince him that there was nothing between Gerry and me. There followed a long tirade about men who were opportunists, who led poor, innocent females astray, until I felt as though I was taking part in a Victorian melodrama. By this time I had ceased to be amused and was very irritated with both my father and with Durrell. Then a hideous thought came into my head. Was Gerry himself seriously under the impression that I wanted to marry him? Well, there was only one thing to do : send a telegram— 'IMPERATIVE YOU PHONE ME IMMEDIATELY REVERSING CHARGES IF NECESSARY.' I thought this economy would incite him.[9] It brought an almost immediate response : 'WILL TELEPHONE YOU TONIGHT.' I hung around that telephone for what seemed like hours, so that by the time Durrell did phone, I was in a furious temper with both him and myself, and I attacked him furiously. How dare he put me in such an awkward position.— There were to be no more letters, postcards, telegrams, and definitely no more parcels. Although I appreciated his kindness to me in the past, it was all getting far beyond the bounds of normal friendship and therefore all communications had to cease.— Poor Durrell could not get a word in edgeways.

'What on earth's happened?' he kept saying, when I allowed him to. I tried to explain about my father's attitude to our association and, much to my chagrin, Gerry was quite sensible about it and said yes, he could quite under-

[8] Unfortunately, up to that point, the truth as far as he was concerned was far from unpleasant. G.D.

[9] This constant harping on my parsimoniousness is difficult to counteract. All I can say is that as the starry-eyed young lover, I would send telegrams of twice the normal length if I knew they were to be paid for at the other end. Can love carry you farther? G.D.

stand my father's concern, and he thought the best thing he could do was to come back as soon as possible and try to straighten everything out. It was useless telling him not to waste his money, as he insisted that it was the least he could do to restore peace and harmony to our household. I rang off just as my father came into the room. I told him what had happened and that Gerry was coming up to see him and would explain it all personally.

'Good, good,' he said, 'I'll make it quite clear to that young man that I don't welcome his attentions towards you. After all, who is he? What is he? What do we know about him? On his own admission he comes from a very dubious background and he certainly has no money, nor is ever likely to have, if I'm any judge of character.'[10]

I again insisted that I was not in the least interested in either Gerry or his prospects, and that he was making a great fuss about nothing.

Two days later the architect of my misfortunes appeared in person, but by this time the whole situation had ceased to amuse me and all I was interested in was restoring peace and quiet. Anxiously I waited whilst my parent and Durrell were closeted together. Instead of the furious outburst that I had half expected, all I heard was apparently peaceful conversation, interspersed with several bursts of loud laughter, and by the time the meeting was over, I was livid.

Smiling happily to himself, Durrell told me that everything was fine.

'What did you say to him?' I asked determinedly.

'Well, I asked your father outright why he objected to our friendship, and he assured me that he had no objections at all, either to me personally or to you coming out with me. His anxiety was merely that of any normal parent who doesn't want a very talented daughter with a seemingly brilliant future to waste time on trivialities.'

[10] The dubious background referred to is presumably my family. While having a certain protective feeling towards them, I must admit that I have spent the greater part of my life endeavouring to live them down. G.D.

I exploded. So my father would rather believe a comparative stranger than me.[11] This was completely contrary to everything he had said to me before. Gerry grabbed me before I could go in pursuit of him.

'Now, now, calm down, the poor man is genuinely worried, but I think I've convinced him that although I would very much like to marry you I've no intention of pressing my suit where it's unwelcome.'

'Thank you very much,' I said, 'but where does this leave me?'

'Well, it's up to you, isn't it?'

'When are you going back to Bournemouth?'

'Oh, in a couple of days' time. After all, if your father doesn't object to my taking you out, I might as well take advantage of it.'

I was really very hurt by my father's attitude. After all the shouting and the fuss, he had backed down. Well, I would really give him something to worry about. He thought I was seriously involved with Gerry and might run off and marry him—well, I would be.

Gerry was easily persuaded to stay on a little longer, and I went out of my way to be with him as much as possible, staying out until all hours and watching my father's face with much satisfaction, for I could see that he was furious and yet unable to say anything in view of his conversation with Gerry.

There was one thing, however, that neither of us had reckoned with. I had entered into this game as a way of getting back at stupidity, but I suddenly found that our attitude to each other had changed. Having spent every spare minute together, it soon began to dawn on us that we were getting emotionally involved and that it would not be easy to say goodbye. Another thing that was quite clear to us both was that the situation was impossible.

[11] The use of the phrase 'comparative stranger' is interesting since, on her own admission, we had (so far as the rather damp and unexciting environs of Manchester allowed) been on fairly intimate terms for a fair length of time. G.D.

There was no prospect of our being able to marry, for I was under age and Gerry's finances were at their lowest—his total assets were £200 and no job. On top of this, his health began to deteriorate, and as he had nearly died of malignant malaria two years previously, even my father was worried. Gerry and I spent hours discussing our predicament, and it was decided that the best thing to do was for Gerry to try to get a job. This would not be easy, as he only knew about animals and zoo jobs were always difficult to get. Anyway, he would write to various zoos and to people who might be able to help.

So began a most agonising period, and, to help matters out, Gerry went back to Bournemouth until something definite was resolved about his future. Our only contact now was by letter and the occasional telephone conversation.

By now I was twenty-one and so did not need my father's permission to marry, but Gerry was still adamant that he had to get a job of some kind.[12] Things were getting really difficult at home and so I was delighted when I received an invitation to visit Gerry's sister in Bournemouth. She was going to get married again and thought it might be a good idea for us all to meet, especially as Gerry and I were now definitely going to get married. It took a great deal of persuasion on my part before I was allowed to go to Bournemouth for a long week-end, and Durrell came all the way up to collect me. It was a wonderful trip.

It was late when we got to the house and I shall never forget that meeting. I had never been in a room where what looked like half an orchard was protruding out of the fire. When it burnt down, anyone who was nearby pushed it farther into the grate. At least it was one way of keeping warm, and obviously the large young man sitting next to Margaret wished to expend no energy whatsoever in cutting it up into small pieces. The white walls were covered with brightly coloured oriental rugs and postcards

---

[12] This is a fairly typical symptom of potential wives. I had not the slightest intention, if I could avoid it, of getting a job. G.D.

of the various places that family and friends had visited.
It was all very 'Bohemian'. Sister Margaret was sitting
on a divan, dressed in a long, tartan housecoat. She grinned
at us and told us that her mother had got tired of waiting
up and had gone to bed. Food was in the larder and our
beds had been made up.

We sat around the fire, talking and eating, Margaret
asking us the occasional vague question about what we
planned to do next, especially if Gerry could not find a
job. Like all young hopefuls, we were both optimistic that
something would turn up soon.

'Yes, but just in case it doesn't,' she said casually, 'I've a
suggestion to make. I can't pay you the money I owe you,
Gerry, I'm afraid, but what you could both do is move into
one of my flatlets and live as part of the family. After all,
Mother's leaving us soon to go and live down the road with
Brother Leslie, so there would be room for you without
straining our resources too much. But I don't want to press
you to come to a decision now. Think about it. The room's
there if you want it.'

'Well, it's up to Jacquie. After all, not everyone wants to
start married life by living with weird in-laws,' Gerry
argued.

I felt we were rushing things, and I did not want to be
panicked into anything.

'Can I let you know later?' I asked.

'Of course, take as long as you like. Anyway, you're
probably very tired now,' said Margo, yawning prodigi-
ously, 'and I suggest that we all go to bed.'

It was a long time before I could go to sleep, as all sorts
of arguments kept rushing through my mind. I didn't want
to seem ungrateful, but I barely knew them, and I might
even decide not to marry Gerry after all.[18]

The next thing I knew, Gerry was shaking me and
offering me a cup of tea.

[18] This is pure prevarication. She had decided from the moment
that we met and I had long ago become a mere pawn in her hands.
G.D.

'Now don't feel you've got to get up right away. There's plenty of hot water and I'll be waiting for you downstairs when you're ready.'

I purposely took my time over getting up and having a bath, and I speculated what the rest of the family might be like. I knew that Gerry's mother was a widow, and that there were four children altogether, of whom Gerry was the youngest. All my impressions of the family had been sketched in from what Gerry had said, and I was quite frankly terrified at the thought of meeting them all. Elder Brother Larry seemed the most formidable, but I probably wouldn't meet him yet as he lived abroad. Brother Leslie only lived down the road, though, and he might not approve of me.

'No member of the family ever interferes with another except when he thinks that the other member is doing something wrong—which is most of the time,' Gerry had assured me; but it would be unpleasant to live so close to them if I was not completely accepted.

Bracing myself for the ordeal, I went downstairs. I heard voices coming from the living-room, and as I entered conversation ceased. Quickly, Gerry came over and dragged me towards a tiny, elderly lady who was standing in front of the fire.

'This is my mother,' he said.

I was astonished. She was completely different from how I had imagined her; instead of the tall, rather forbidding woman I had always pictured, here was a tiny, gentle person with merry blue eyes and silver hair. She smiled and shook hands with me.

'Thank God you're not a blonde, dear,' she said grinning wickedly.

Margaret came into the room at this point and they all roared with laughter. Getting bolder, I asked, 'What would you have done if I had been a blonde?'

'Nothing,' replied Mrs. Durrell, 'but I'm relieved just the same.' I gathered later that all her favourite son's past girl-friends had been blonde and blue-eyed—cowlike, is how

Mrs. Durrell described them—and she had an absolute horror of one of them becoming her daughter-in-law.[14]

My meeting with Brother Leslie took place later that day. He came bursting into the living-room, looking for his mother, scowled at me, turned on his heels and went into the kitchen. Gerry brought him back into the room and introduced us. He was a dark-haired man with penetrating blue eyes and, like the rest of the family, apart from Gerry, not much taller than me. He, I decided, was also nice—only one to go.

The whole week-end passed very quickly, and it took all my efforts to drag myself away and return home, this time alone as we thought it might be better for everyone if Gerry stayed away from Manchester while I tried to persuade my father to see reason about our getting married—not that I now needed his permission.

This was quite a harrowing period for it soon became quite obvious that nothing would make my father relent, and in the end he even refused to discuss it with me. On top of this, Gerry was becoming very impatient and was pressing me for a decision one way or the other. Margaret wrote to me in the meantime, renewing her offer of help and adding that Mrs. Durrell would help us out financially until Gerry found something. I felt dreadful—I didn't want to alienate my father or go against his wishes, and yet I felt that this was my one opportunity to break free once and for all and have a life of my own.

Quite suddenly, the whole matter was resolved for me. My father had to go away on business for a few days and Gerry turned up unexpectedly. I had to make up my mind now.

We spent hours discussing the problem and the ways and means of resolving it without hurting anybody, but of course there just was no sensible way of doing this. I tried

[14] My mother, for some reason best known to herself, viewed the selection of exquisite, ethereal females that I brought to the house with some suspicion. In the light of future events, she would have done better to view brunettes with even more suspicion. G.D.

to be logical, pointing out that we could not get married, never mind live on the money that Gerry had left, but he seemed to have an answer for everything. In sheer desperation I called a truce, promising to let him have my final answer within forty-eight hours. I desperately wanted to say yes, but many things worried me. Apart from our lack of money—and I knew my father would give me nothing if I married against his wishes—there was the question of temperament. We had absolutely nothing in common and once the first flush of enthusiasm in being together was over, would it be a lasting relationship?[15] I had a very promising career but this would all have to go if I got married. It was obvious that Gerry needed someone who shared his interests and would be willing to go abroad on trips with him and take part wholly in whatever he wanted to do, and I was not prepared to do this.[16] On the other hand, he was an amusing and charming companion and someone I felt I could utterly rely upon, and I began to convince myself that we could work out a compromise.

Durrell kept his part of the agreement and never even mentioned marriage for the next two days. As our truce period came to an end, we decided to go out and see a film and have supper, so that by the time we got back to the house we were in fairly high spirits. It was quite late and everyone else had gone to bed, so we had the living-room to ourselves. We just sat there in the warmth and talked, but not about marriage. Suddenly I felt very tired and was horrified to see that it was five o'clock. In our mad rush to get out of the door we both somehow got jammed in the doorway, and as we were disentangling ourselves Gerry said very quietly, 'Well, will you marry me?'[17]

[15] I could never understand this business of people having something in common when they married and having lasting relationships. After all, there was the bed to be made, meals to be cooked and the whole tenor of life to be kept on an even keel. What more could a girl want? G.D.

[16] Ha, ha. G.D.

[17] This is a remarkably cold description of what I would always consider to be a very poignant scene. However, since my wife assures

As my resistance is always at its lowest ebb at that hour of the morning, I said, 'Yes, of course I will,' and so the trouble was over.

Having at last made my decision, I never permitted any doubts to enter my mind. Our marriage was obviously going to be a great success and therefore all apparent obstacles would disappear. The fact that we had by now barely £40 to get married on did not deter me in the least. Carefully we worked it all out. The special licence would cost about £3; then there were the train tickets to Bournemouth, sundries like taxis, cartage of luggage and the wedding ring; yes, there would be more than enough. Naturally, there was no question of an engagement ring or a honeymoon, and somehow it did not worry us—after all, getting married was the chief thing.

In view of the imminent return of my papa, we decided to beat a hasty retreat and go down to Bournemouth to get married; even living in Bournemouth would be like a honeymoon.[18]

Trade Union activity has never particularly interested me, but the threat of a railway strike caused us to accelerate our departure. The next twenty-four hours were filled with pushing my personal belongings—books, music, records, plus all the junk[19] that Gerry had managed to accumulate —into tea chests and any other thing that we could press into service. Halfway through, I began to have doubts

---

me that we don't want this book banned, I draw a discreet veil over it, only registering my protest in a minor key. G.D.

[18] This statement shows that I only rescued her in the nick of time from the awful peasant squalor that pervades the life of anybody living north of a line drawn from Bristol to London. The fact that she actually imagined that living in Bournemouth would be like a honeymoon is condemnation in itself. G.D.

[19] I take strong objection to the word 'junk'. A genuine Mandrill's skull, several ju-ju dolls and an extraordinarily interesting beer mug that played 'God Save the King' as you drank out of it, could not be considered 'junk' by any right-thinking person. G.D.

that we would ever get away. Two taxis were ordered for the crack of dawn the next day and we prayed that all our stuff would fit into them, but despite the large array of trunks, boxes and cases, there were still a lot of things to be put into something, so I desperately began making up a series of brown-paper parcels, and by the time we had packed up the last thing it was three o'clock in the morning.

During all this fevered activity my step-mother became more and more agitated, for she was the one who would have to face my irate father on his return.

'Don't worry, I've left a letter for him and I strongly advise you to give it to him before he actually misses me. In this way you can avert the storm—with luck.'

Naturally, this did not give her very much comfort.

'All you have got to do is blame it all on to me,' I said, with all the confidence of one who is leaving. 'Tell him that I was stubborn and wouldn't listen to you. Emphasise how you pleaded with me to have sense and respect my father's views, and, above all, tell him how you begged me to wait until his return and tell him myself.' I just did not care how she blackened me—I knew I would not be popular anyway. I left her to it.

How I dragged myself out of bed after only three hours' sleep, I will never know, but we eventually stuffed ourselves into our waiting taxis and started on our journey. It was a miserable morning, grey, gloomy and wet and hardly the right atmosphere for a gay elopement, but I was far too tired to care about anything except getting on that damned train.

After a lot of tearing around the station, Gerry finally captured one of these elusive beasts, a porter. He was neither in the first flush of youth nor in a very good temper, but he did eventually appear with a truck and piled all our stuff on it, sweetly bypassing the weighing machine and trundling off towards the London platform, while we two brought up the rear, carrying all the paper parcels and brandishing a reading lamp. We must have looked a little odd at that hour of the morning for our appearance seemed to create a mild sensation as we meandered amongst all those soberly dressed business types.

The elderly guard had been watching us walk down the platform and had shown our porter where to stow the luggage. As we drew level with him he looked at us mournfully.

'Are you two getting married?' he queried.

Struggling with my bursting parcels I replied, 'Yes.'

'Well, Gawd 'elp yer,' he said, and waved his flag.[20]

CHAPTER 2

Our eventual arrival in Bournemouth later that day was startling in comparison to the gloom that we had left behind, and it was a great relief to me to be with people who whole-heartedly approved of both of us and our marriage. The entire family had gathered to meet us and were all bubbling over with enthusiasm, vying with each other to gain our attention. Mrs. Durrell told us that she had just received a letter from Larry—he was in the Foreign Service in Jugoslavia—and, strangely enough, that he too approved of the whole thing. This seemed to set a seal on the proceedings although Margo protested that Larry's opinion did not matter anyway; still, it was nice to have the approval of the head of the family.

'Now then, dear,' said Mrs. Durrell, turning to Gerry, 'what ideas have you about your wedding?'

'Well, Jacquie and I feel that it ought to take place as soon as possible, just in case her Papa appears with a shotgun,' Gerry said.

So the next day was Operation Wedding Day and each member of the family was dispersed over Bournemouth to arrange things. Gerry and I hunted for the registry office,

[20] The guard was right of course, but then fortunately He has. G.D.

where we were interviewed by a charming woman who seemed very reluctant to believe that I was over twenty-one despite my birth certificate, and it was arranged that the actual ceremony would take place on 26th February. Margaret had appointed herself head of the Commissariat and promised to supply all the eats, including the wedding cake, while Mrs. Durrell and Leslie took it upon themselves to see that there was plenty to drink. When we announced that we were to be married in three days' time, the women, contrary to our expectations, were appalled. How on earth were they to get everything ready in time, they moaned.

'Oh, don't worry,' said Gerry, 'it will be all right.'

Poor Margo, in despair, rushed out of the house, leaving instructions that we were to meet her for tea at 3.30, as she would need reviving after having done battle with the cake shop. Naturally, she was not there when we reached the restaurant but soon she appeared, beaming, and sat down with a self-satisfied air.

'How did you get on, Margo?' asked Gerry.

'What a time I've had,' she said, 'trying to persuade that wretched cake shop to produce a wedding cake within twenty-four hours.'

'Well, go on, tell us what happened.'

She had walked in and smilingly ordered a single-tier wedding cake.

'Certainly, Madam, and when is it for?'

'Monday,' replied Margaret.

'What!' gasped the assistant, 'but it's impossible.'

'I know it's very short notice, but it's rather an unusual wedding, all very romantic. You see, they've eloped.'

This apparently made all the difference, and soon everyone in the shop knew and expressed their delight at playing their part in this great romance. 'How nice', 'how unusual', 'you often read about such things in the newspapers but you never actually dream of one taking place in the same town and your knowing all about it.'

'Anyway,' concluded Margaret, laughing, 'they promised faithfully to deliver it on time and they made me promise to congratulate you both.'

As a reward for her efforts we ordered large slabs of cream gâteau, which Margaret devoured with obvious pleasure.

'Now then, Gerry, what about a wedding ring?' said Margaret, getting all efficient again. 'Let's go and have a look at some.'

Eventually we settled on a modest, slim, octagonal gold ring which, the very practical assistant in the jeweller's carefully pointed out, would not wear well if Madam was doing housework. But I liked it and, who knows, we might be able to afford a new ring later on.[1] More of our precious pounds were handed over, and in a final fling of extravagance we all piled into a taxi, stopping on the way to order some flowers—a bouquet for me and a few floral tributes for the house. The whole atmosphere was absurd. Everyone else was thrilled and excited, whilst Gerry and I were carrying on like an ancient married couple, accepting things quite calmly and almost as though they were our right.

The next two days were taken up with getting the little flatlet ready. Although it was a tiny room at the back of the house, it really was charming. It overlooked the large back garden, and in the distance we could see the heather-covered heights of St. Catherine's Head. Wood pigeons and other wild birds hovered around the pine trees and I really felt that I was at last living in the country. Margo had furnished the room quite simply but it was very cosy, especially when we lit the fire in the little grate. The room itself was just large enough to take a double bed, a small desk, a single wardrobe, a chest-of-drawers and one fireside chair. It really was fun, installing all our belongings in this room, although Gerry was in a flutter about his books; but

[1] You can see the mercenary element creeping in here and we weren't even properly churched. G.D.

Margo soon solved this problem by reappearing with a book-case which just fitted on top of the chest-of-drawers, and she also installed a tiny bedside table and lamp. There was no need to worry about cooking facilities at this stage, as we were all going to eat downstairs.

Into the middle of this small upheaval strolled Margaret's first husband, Jack Breeze.

'Just the man we want,' said Gerry. 'We're getting married tomorrow, so why don't you be our best man or whatever it is that one needs at a registry office? Oh, and by the way, this is the person I'm going to marry,' he added, pushing me forward.

'You poor thing,' said Jack, 'how did you get embroiled with the Durrells?' Raising one of his bushy eyebrows, he asked, 'You didn't have to, did you?' and then roared with laughter.

'Of course I'll be in attendance, Gerry. I wouldn't miss this for the world, though you mustn't expect me to give you a wedding present. What with all the responsibilities and children and wives I have I can't afford to throw away my hard-earned on providing fripperies for you lot.'

I soon came to learn that Jack always carried on as though he was a pauper, and it was now a family joke, but like all people who are supposedly Scrooge-like he was in fact the most generous soul.

On the Sunday night we held a small family party in lieu of the traditional bachelor fling and so it was a very subdued group that presented itself at the registry office the following day. It was, without doubt, the dreariest day, grey and muggy.

We must have looked peculiar, for it was quite obvious that neither Gerry nor I had new clothes for this special occasion. We had no money to spare and we just had to make do with what we already had. Still, I did try to follow the old adage—something old (my coat), something new (a pair of nylons), a present from a friend, something borrowed (a blouse from Margaret), something blue (a scarf). Durrell looked quite neat and tidy and had even cleaned his shoes, a really startling phenomenon.[2]

The ceremony was quite short. I remember wondering what on earth I was doing, getting myself involved in all this, but I recovered enough to agree that I would accept Gerald Malcolm as my lawful wedded husband, and soon it was all over and we were on our way back to the house. Gerry smiled and squeezed my hand.

'It's too late,' he said, 'I've got you now.'[3]

Although our party was a small one, nothing was omitted. Speeches were made, toasts were proposed, and the cake, which had arrived that morning as promised, was cut and distributed. A great deal of teasing and leg-pulling was indulged in, and it was quite obvious that everyone had enjoyed themselves.

There never was any question of our having a honeymoon for we had no money left, but this to me was a relief and I was quite happy that our life should revolve entirely around our small room and the family. Naturally, our pleasures were simple, but we were never bored or restricted in any way. There were masses of books to read, lovely country for us to walk in, and dear Jack Breeze had given us an old radio.

Our money was running out and so I had to take stock of the situation, help Gerry devise some plan of campaign, and also, which was far more important, plan our expenditure, such as it was. So far, Gerry had two main vices—cigarettes and tea drinking—and I was determined that

---

[2] These are the sort of snide remarks which form the most corrosive element in any marriage. The implication that I never cleaned my shoes is entirely erroneous. To prove it I have the dates on which I cleaned my shoes during that year noted down in my diary. This is the foretaste of married life : The few tiny pebbles that foretell the avalanche of criticism and condemnation which you are letting yourself in for. G.D.

[3] Without wishing to be too unkind and, while prepared, at a pinch, to admit that my memory may be at fault, I was under the strong impression that what I actually said was 'It's too late. You've got me now.' G.D.

whatever happened he was not going to give these up. Our
first major problem was to get Gerry a job. All his efforts
to get one in England had failed, so we decided that we
ought to look farther afield, perhaps to Africa, with one
of the game departments, or even emigrate to Australia.
As we could not afford to buy those newspapers that normally carry official advertisements, we made a daily pilgrim-
age to the Central Library Reading Room. The jobs that
were open to a man like Gerry, who had neither academic
qualifications nor commercial training, were limited, but we
hoped that something in the animal line would offer itself
before too long. Apart from this we took the names and
addresses of all the zoos in Australia, America and Canada,
and over the next few weeks a stream of letters poured
forth, enclosing a short résumé of Durrell's achievements to
date, which were not inconsiderable for such a young man.
Then began weeks of anxiety while we waited for the
replies. Surprisingly, not many zoos even had the courtesy
to acknowledge the letters, and the few that did reply
could offer nothing. As an investment this had all been a
dead loss. I was not despondent, however, but just plain
mad, and we carried on with our paper gazing.

About this time a former associate of Gerry's asked if we
would like to look after a seaside menagerie that he was in
charge of at Margate. He could not afford to pay us a
salary but would cover the cost of our lodging and our food,
plus our fares. Durrell leapt at the opportunity of getting
back to working with animals again.

'And anyway,' he said, 'it will be a good training ground
for you.'

'But I don't know anything about keeping animals,' I
protested.

'Well, you'll soon learn.'

The little zoo was part of a seaside fun-fair and was half
aquarium and half animals. Soon I was deeply involved in
skinning bananas, peeling oranges, de-stoning cherries,
bottle-feeding babies and generally learning about animal
keeping the hard way. I now realise why it is a much

respected rule that one should never be taught anything by one's husband. I was spared nothing.[4]

'I can't get all the muck off the bottom of this cage,' I complained.

'Well, use your hands then,' was the only help I ever got.

Although it was exhausting and wearing work, I would not have missed those three weeks for anything, and I began to appreciate the fun of looking after wild animals. I was not sorry, though, to return to Bournemouth.

In between cutting up fruit and cleaning cages I had had time to concentrate on our future and an idea had begun to germinate. Larry Durrell was quite a successful author and had, from all accounts, always encouraged Gerry to write. If one Durrell could write and make money at it, why should another one not try? So began Operation Nag. Poor Durrell suffered. For days I went on and on about him writing something for somebody.

'I can't write, at least not like Larry.'

'How do you know you can't write until you try?' and in sheer desperation poor Durrell began to put some ideas down on paper.

'What can I write about, anyway?'

'Well, about these trips you've been on.'

'Who on earth wants to know about all that?'

'I do, so get on with it.'

Larry was due in England with his wife, Eve. She was expecting their first child and it was agreed that she should have it in England rather than in Jugoslavia. Although a meeting with the genius of the family was a bit awe-inspiring, I must admit that he was far nicer than I had ever imagined. Larry was small and stocky and instantly recognisable as a Durrell, with all the Durrell charm and humour, though far more sophisticated and suave. Both he and Eve were very sweet and kind to me, and Larry was very concerned about Gerry not being able to get a job.

'Why on earth don't you write a book about these dread-

[4] In actual fact, she had a very light basic training, but women do like to exaggerate these things. G.D.

ful trips you go on, and make some money for a change?
After all, the British simply love stories about fluffy animals
and jungles, and it's so easy to do—you've got ample
material and what-have-you.'

Gerry was quite obviously not eager to pursue this conversation, but he felt me glaring at him.

'Perhaps I could write a book about my three trips,
although it would probably be ghastly.'

'My dear boy, you are not seriously suggesting that you
write three trips up as one book, are you?' Larry said in
horror. 'You must be mad. Surely to heaven you can get a
book out of each one?'

'You know, I don't honestly think so, Larry. Remember,
I've had no experience of serious writing. It's all right
for you, you love it and you've been writing for years,
whereas I find it a bore even writing letters. Ask Mother
here how many times I wrote to her while I was away.'

'It's not the same at all. Anyway, why not try it and see?
I'm willing to read the first few chapters and give you an
honest opinion, even though I don't know much about
animal books. Also, I'm more than prepared to give you an
introduction to my publishers, Fabers. Take my advice,
don't bother with agents; they cheat you and take your
money for nothing, and only put themselves out when you
are a success.'

It was more than obvious that Durrell was not at all keen
on this 'good, sound advice', but I was determined that he
should at least try it. Later that week we listened to a rather
dreary talk on the radio about life in West Africa. After
many moans from Durrell, I said, 'If you think you can
do something better than that, why not do a talk for the
B.B.C. about West Africa?'

'That's not writing as Larry means it, you know,' he
said.

'Of course, I do, but it's a start and at least it's one way
of making some money,' I persisted.

'Anyway, what could I write a radio talk about?'

I was getting irritated.

'Oh, stop being so defeatist, Gerry, and at least try. After all, you keep me amused for hours with stories about the Africans and all the animals you collected, so why not have a go at conveying all this to the listeners. Promise me that you'll do it. At least it's better than rotting here.'

Nothing more was said about this for several days, then I heard Gerry asking Margo if one of her friends could lend him a typewriter.

'Jack's got an old one, I know. Why don't you ask him when he gets back? If he felt you wanted to make money with it, I'm sure he would lend it to you.'

Suddenly Durrell decided that he could not wait for Jack's return, he needed a typewriter now. They cost about 30/- a week to hire, which we just did not have to spare; there was nothing for it, we would have to get rid of some of Gerry's books, some of which were quite valuable. The sale of these precious things seemed to spur Durrell on, and he began to make notes about his African trips, listing the various things that might be a suitable subject for a radio talk.

'I've got it,' he announced grandly one morning. 'I'm going to write about the Hairy Frog and how I caught it. The only problem is, how many words go to a fifteen minute script.'

'There must be some way of finding out.'

Somewhere in the house, we knew, was a copy of the *Writers' and Artists' Yearbook* which had originally belonged to Larry, and eventually it was run to earth by Mrs. Durrell among the books that she had taken with her to Leslie's house. Closeted in our small room, supported by an endless series of pots of tea, Durrell tentatively launched himself on 'The Hunt for the Hairy Frog', and as each page was finished it was passed to me for approval and correcting of the many spelling mistakes. It was a startling fact that no member of the Durrell family could spell, despite their public school educations, and it was Mrs. Durrell's proud boast that she, who had gone to a very small American school in India, could out-spell all her expensively educated offspring. I became engrossed in the story of the strange amphibian with thick hair-like filaments on its hind legs, that Gerry had found, captured and brought back to the London Zoo, and I simply could not wait for the pages to roll off the typewriter. To save time and Gerry's two fingers, I evolved a simple way of correcting spelling mistakes, typing the corrections on to sticky paper which was then cut out and stuck over the offending word. It was naturally a tedious business but it did get the damned thing finished, and finally all that was left to do was to send it off to the B.B.C. Talks Department in London, and hope. Our normal occupation of post watching acquired an added zest—at least for me it did. Durrell was just not interested.

One morning, for no apparent reason, Durrell suddenly said :

'Why don't you have a hair cut? I'm getting tired of you looking like a central European refugee,' and before I could do anything, he and Margo dragged me into the bathroom brandishing a pair of scissors and started attacking my flowing locks, completely ignoring my protests and refusing to let me look in a mirror. They went on hacking and hacking until I began to feel bald. When they eventually approved of their handiwork, they allowed me to look in the mirror. Much to my surprise the result was quite presentable, and my short hair cut was later made very popular by Audrey Hepburn in 'Sabrina Fair'. Since then many people have tried to persuade me to let it grow long again, but Durrell won't have it, and on looking at old photographs I cannot say I blame him.

'You do realise, don't you, that Larry has had many things rejected, so don't pin your faith on one little talk,' was all my dear spouse could comfort me with.

At last it came, not a rejection slip but a most charming letter from a Mr. Radley, inviting Gerry to ring him up about the script. We rushed down to Leslie's house to show the letter to everyone, and also to use the telephone. We could hardly believe it; not only did they like the script very much indeed, but they wanted to broadcast it soon, and they wanted Gerry to read it himself.

The broadcast was a great success. Gerry was assured by everyone that he was a natural broadcaster, and if he could write such good scripts then the Talks Department would always be willing to have them. But what pleased me even more was a cheque for fifteen guineas. This finally persuaded Durrell that perhaps there was some sense in Larry's idea and that he ought to try his hand at a book about his first African trip. He already had a suitable title—*The Overloaded Ark*—and all he had to do now was write the wretched thing.

Thus began a rather weird existence for us both. Because Durrell found it far easier to write at night when there was nothing around to disturb him, he decided to become nocturnal. This put a great strain on our relationship. We were confined in a very small space, I was an extremely light sleeper, unable to bear even the slightest sound, but we needed money so we had to adjust. Just when our meagre funds were at their lowest ebb and we were having to part with our hired typewriter, dear Jack came to our rescue and lent us his portable until the epic was finished. As this machine was far quieter than the hired model, I was doubly grateful to Jack.

Durrell worked on this book as I had never known him work, and every morning there was a pile of pages for me to read and correct, and slowly the book began to take shape. We were both consumed with excitement, and again I found myself completely engrossed in the story, which was surprising as I had always loathed animal-travel books, but this was quite different from anything I had ever read before and I began to have a sneaking feeling that it might make us quite a lot of money. It went on and on and on, and it began to look as if Gerry was trying to write *Gone With the Wind*.

'How many words should it be, Gerry?' I asked one morning.

'Oh, about 60,000 I think.'

'Well, don't you think it would be rather a good idea if I started to count them for you?'

'Okay, if you want to.'

'Gerry,' I said later, 'you'd better finish soon, you've already written 65,000.'

'Jolly good,' he said, 'you can have the last chapter tomorrow morning.'

The next stage was to sew all the pages together between two end pieces of stiff cardboard, type a label with the title and Gerry's name and the address and the number of words on it, and wrap it up into a neat parcel. On Larry's advice we sent it to Alan Pringle at Fabers' with a covering note just to remind him who it was from. Thankfully we consigned it to Her Majesty's mails. We were both so weary and exhausted by our efforts that all we wanted to do now was sleep and forget it, and in any case Larry had warned us that it would be weeks before we heard anything further from the publishers.

About this time two possible jobs came up, one in the Uganda Game Department and the other in the Khartoum Museum in the Sudan. In spite of the manuscript Gerry went to interviews for both the situations but rejected the Sudan job immediately because he could not take me with him for at least two years. The Uganda job was, however, quite different and he felt quite confident of getting it. That is, until the Conservative Government was returned, introduced various economies, and Gerry's job disappeared almost overnight. He was furious, but, as I gaily pointed out, would he still want to be a game ranger in the middle of Uganda if he turned out to be a successful author?

'That's not the point,' he insisted. 'God knows if we'll ever have this book accepted, and if we do it might only make a few pounds.'

'Well, we'll see,' I replied confidently.

Fabers' wrote to us a month later, saying that they liked

the manuscript very much and could Gerry come to see
them in London to talk about it? This was not easy, for
once again lack of funds was very pressing. Gerry had no
photographs of the exotic animals in the book, and it was
trying to have to discuss illustrations. Finally Fabers'
offered to pay a Swiss artist to do the drawings, and six
weeks after they had first received the manuscript it was
agreed that they would handle serial and translation rights,
etc., in the normal way and would pay us an advance of
£100, £50 on signature of the contract and £50 three
months later. It was now April 1952.

While we were waiting for publication day we still had to
live, and with his new-found enthusiasm Durrell managed to
produce a few articles for various magazines and a couple
of radio talks. Nevertheless, we were still desperately short
of money. The feeling that perhaps Larry was wrong about
literary agents really worried us, to such an extent that we
decided to go to see Larry's own agent, Spencer Curtis
Brown, and ask for his advice.

Our first approach was naturally by letter, briefly out-
lining what had happened so far and asking if he would
read the book. Mr. Curtis Brown replied almost immediately, asking for a copy of the manuscript. So Fabers' were
asked to supply a galley proof. A few days later we received
another letter—would Gerry go to London to see him?
Once again we descended on Leslie's house to use the
telephone. We could not afford a trip to London and I
insisted that Gerry told Curtis Brown so. The whole family
waited anxiously in the living-room for Gerry to finish
his call.

'What do you think?' he burst into the room. 'He's so
anxious to see me that he's sending me some money to
travel with.'

This was fantastic and it really was the first time that
anyone had given us any concrete evidence of their faith in
Gerry's abilities. We most certainly got a cheque from him
—not to cover the cost of the fare, but for £120. This was

from a man who was part of the hated fraternity of literary agents and who had not earned one penny from any of Gerry's work.

'I could kick myself for allowing Larry to put me off going to a literary agent,' Gerry moaned. 'I must have been raving mad, but I've learnt my lesson and I'll certainly never do it again, even if Curtis Brown won't handle me.'

Durrell insisted that I went with him to London.

'After all,' he said, 'you know I'll never remember anything at all of what's said to me. In fact, I'll probably forget the man's name.'

Having spent nearly eighteen months in a small room in Bournemouth, it was a double pleasure for me to go up to London.

'Let's be really extravagant and take a taxi. After all, we don't know where Henrietta Street is and we mustn't be late to meet our benefactor.'

The Curtis Brown offices were right near to Covent Garden Market and at that time housed in a very quaint old building. Spencer Curtis Brown's personal office was at the front of the building and was light and spacious. He was forty-ish and had gingery hair and a military moustache.

'How nice to see you both. Now then, let's talk about your problems.'

He apparently liked the book very much indeed and felt it might prove to be a valuable property if handled correctly.

'If Fabers' haven't placed the American rights yet,' he said, 'can I have your permission to show your manuscript to an American friend of mine I'm having dinner with this evening? I'll certainly get Fabers' approval before doing anything. Anyway, dear boy, leave things with me and I'll see what can be done.'

He refused to be thanked for his cheque.

'It was nothing,' he insisted.

Back in Bournemouth, I was carried off to bed with a rather vicious attack of the 'flu and was feeling very sorry for myself, hating the world and everyone in it. I heard someone running up the stairs and the door burst open. It was Gerry.

'Here's some medicine that should make you feel better,' he said, thrusting a telegram at me.

HAVE SOLD AMERICAN RIGHTS FOR £500 ADVANCE CONGRATULATIONS SPENCER.

We were on our way.

CHAPTER 3

Encouraged by Spencer Curtis Brown, Durrell pushed on with his second book, this time about his trip to British Guiana. Spencer had, quite sensibly, suggested that Gerry finish the book even if *The Overloaded Ark* had not been launched upon the public yet, for if the first book was a success it was a good thing, psychologically, to have another one ready for immediate publication. We all realised, of course, that under the terms of the first contract Fabers' would have to have first refusal on the new book, but we were also equally determined that they would have to pay a great deal more by way of an advance.

It seemed that everything was now running in our favour, and after two years of scrimping and saving we could, at last, relax a little. The new book, *Three Singles to Adventure*, was a very light-hearted affair and was too full, I thought, of schoolboy humour, but Spencer liked it and this time we nagged a friend into typing it for us, so there was no sticky paper routine to indulge in. The nocturnal system was again used; our friend kept pace with Gerry's output and, as a result, the book was finished completely in just over six weeks. As if to underline our new-found confidence, *The Overloaded Ark* was a Book

Society Choice and a *Daily Mail* Book of the Month. Before this, Fabers' had not at first agreed to pay on *Three Singles* alone the advance stipulated by Spencer, and Hart-Davis had eagerly offered to take Gerry over; when Fabers' equalled his offer to settle the matter, there had been arbitration—joint publication, or Hart-Davis. So began our long and happy association with Rupert Hart-Davis and Ralph Thompson, who has since illustrated nearly all Gerry's books.

Money poured in, or so it seemed, so we could now think seriously of going away on an animal collecting trip. As a special treat, I was allowed to decide which country it should be. For some unknown reason the Argentine had always exercised a peculiar fascination for me, and so without hesitation I decided that this was the place.

Durrell, of course, was carried away by the thought of South America and had visions of embracing Chile and perhaps Paraguay in our itinerary. Brother Larry gave us a word of warning—anything to do with South America must be negotiated at top diplomatic level, especially in the Argentine, for he knew only too well the Latin American love of red tape from his own sojourn there as a British Consul Representative.

'This is a perfect opportunity for you to find out what it's really like, preparing for one of these trips,' announced Durrell, 'so to you can go the privilege of writing the letters.'

'Thanks,' I replied, 'I'm deeply grateful.'

Apart from the preparation for this trip, Gerry was also in the middle of writing his third book, *The Bafut Beagles*, for again, as Spencer had pointed out, Gerry would not feel like writing a book immediately after returning from a long trip, and Hart-Davis were anxious to keep up with the demand for Durrell books, all of which made us lots of lovely money.

Things really began to move now; what with Durrell trying to write a book as well as organise an expedition and deal with a mass of other things, it was quite obvious, even to me, that we just could not cope single-handed and that we desperately needed a secretary. But where to find anyone dim-witted enough to get involved with us, that was the problem. A Russian friend came to our rescue on hearing of our plight.

'I know someone who runs a small secretarial school. She often gets ex-secretaries coming to her in order to brush up their shorthand-typing, and I seem to remember that they often ask her if she knows of any suitable jobs.'

'I don't want a dizzy youngster without any brains,' Durrell said, 'but an older woman who knows what she's doing and who can be relied upon to turn up every day and, what is more important, adapt herself to my zany working methods—in fact, a saint.'[1]

A few days later the phone rang.

'Gerry, I think I've found the very person for you. Could you possibly go to my friend's house this afternoon and meet the would-be secretary?'

'Naturally,' said Gerry.

Durrell returned about an hour later, full of beans.

'Well, I think I've found the perfect person. She's about forty, quiet and rather shy, and I think she's foreign, probably a refugee. Anyway, she's coming round here in the morning on a three-day trial basis; this was her suggestion, incidentally, as she felt that she mightn't be quick enough and we mightn't like her. Personally, I found her charming and I think she is just being modest about her abilities.'

'She's not going to work in this room, is she?' I asked. 'She'll go mad.'

'No, it's all right, I've arranged with Margo to let her work in the empty flat next door, at least until the end of the week when the new tenants come in.'

'Well, it's a good idea to break her in slowly,' I laughed,

---

[1] There is a slight misrepresentation of facts here. What I would have liked was a slim and extremely attractive blonde who sympathised with me in my unfortunate marriage, but it was not to be. G.D.

'before she has to come face to face with the regiments of empty bottles and tea leaves in our room.'

I could hardly wait to meet this woman who had had the courage to take on Durrell and his works, yet I do not think that any of us were quite prepared for anyone like Sophie. She was of medium height, with unruly dark, wiry hair, pale skin and the most wonderfully placid expression. At first she seemed terrified of us all, but she slowly relaxed as Gerry carefully explained about the manuscript and how many copies were needed, and we left her to it, only interrupting her occasionally to see if she would like a cup of tea.

'I think she's absolutely sweet,' I said, 'and if she can put up with us she'll be perfect.'

Apparently Sophie liked the work very much but still wanted to work her three days as agreed before coming to any final decision. She looked a bit overwhelmed the next morning when she found that she had to work in our tiny room, as the new tenants of the other flat had decided to move in two days early.

'Well,' I thought, 'this will definitely put her off.'

'I've tried to clear a space for you,' I explained, pushing away the inevitable tea tray and ashtrays piled high with fag ends, 'but if you can't manage, please push more things away, for Gerry always swears he knows exactly where everything is.'[2]

Sophie calmly surveyed the room, which now looked rather like the Municipal Rubbish Dump. In addition to our normal debris, we had odd bits of equipment lying around, and one could hardly get into the door anyway, because of the boxes and cases piled high on the landing outside.

'If you need anything just bang on the floor, as I shall

[2] Although, up until then, it had been an uphill struggle, I had managed to remember roughly where the things I wanted lay in the topography of the room; I was completely defeated by a combination of Jacquie and Sophie at this point. I always look on this stage as the beginning of the end. G.D.

be in the kitchen cooking lunch,' and I hastily left her to cope with the latest Durrell epic. Much later, Sophie confided in me that she was highly amused by the sudden change in her circumstances and felt quite at home in the middle of all that muddle. I do not think she ever realised how much sympathy she got from everyone else in the house—that is, except Durrell, who thought it was jolly good basic training for any secretary to get to know us as we really were.

At the end of three days we were determined not to let her go, and fortunately Sophie wanted to stay, providing we could work in with the other arrangements that she had to make. She carefully explained that at the moment she was house-hunting to find a suitable place to bring her ancient mama and brother. Their house in Essex had already been sold so it was imperative that she find somewhere to live very soon. Naturally, we did not mind how she worked as long as the work was finished, and she could come and go as she pleased. This was followed by the most difficult conversation I have ever had in my life. I honestly do not think I have ever met anyone who was so absolutely disinterested in money, and it was with the utmost difficulty that I finally persuaded her to accept something approaching a living wage.[3] She is still the same today, which makes life very difficult, although she cannot understand my despair. We soon came to know and appreciate our find. She was a dear, and was constantly amazing us by doing the most unexpected things. Coming back from London once, after a brief, three-day visit, we found to our amazement that our small flat was spotless. There was a note in the typewriter :

'Dear Bossy, had no work left to do so thought I would give you a nice surprise. Do hope you can find everything. Sophie Cook.'

We were overwhelmed and Durrell, typically, immedi-

---

[3] Jacquie would not adopt my suggestion that we ask Sophie to work for nothing, which I thought was the simplest way out of the *impasse*. G.D.

ately attacked everyone, demanding to know why his secretary had been allowed to do all this housework; after all, it was not her job.

'Do be sensible, dear,' said Mother, 'how on earth could I stop her? Anyway, you ought to be glad that she's so thoughtful.'

All I felt was guilty and I made a determined effort to try and keep the place a lot tidier so that poor Sophie did not feel obliged to clean up the moment we turned our backs. On her next visit Gerry told Sophie quite firmly that, much as we appreciated her kind gesture, she was not, in any circumstances, to do it again.

'But why, Gerry?' she demanded. 'I had nothing left to type and I suddenly thought how nice it would be for you both to come back to a tidy room. It didn't take very long, you know, and I enjoyed doing it.'

'Well, you're not to make a habit of it. It was sweet of you but you're employed as my secretary and not my char.'

'I'm like that, Gerry, I don't like to sit around taking a person's money for doing nothing. You'll get used to me, think nothing of it, my dears.'

From then on until we actually left for the Argentine, Sophie became a vital part of our life, and it was difficult to remember what it had been like without her. Her wonderful sense of humour, which bordered on the ridiculous at times, helped to lighten the whole atmosphere and take away a little of the strain and tension that we were all working under. She told the most outrageous stories of her house-hunting forays; how she peered into every corner for woodworm and dry rot and was quite obviously the bane of every house agent's existence. Her poor mother was getting desperate in Essex and we despaired of her ever finding anything that would be suitable, but finally the day dawned when she actually announced that she had found a house. Of course, it was not really what she wanted, but it would do.

Meanwhile our plans for actually going away had gathered momentum, and it was amazing how helpful complete strangers were to us. These included people like the then Argentine Ambassador, Dr. Derisi, the entire personnel of the Argentinian Consulate in London, the British Consul, the Foreign Office—none of them could do enough for us. Contrary to everyone's expectations we managed to find a ship at a ridiculously low price, which should have warned us what to expect, but I am afraid we were completely carried away by what we were going to do once we got to the country itself. Durrell was especially anxious that I should enjoy the voyage out for two reasons : First, I had never been beyond Europe before, but, far more important, we had never had a honeymoon and he thought that this would, in some way, make up for that.

The days were crammed with letter writing, checking the manuscript of *The Bafut Beagles* before Sophie finally typed it, hurried trips to London to see various officials, and buying equipment for the trip—and, sandwiched in between all this, buying suitable clothing. This was a particular problem, as we were going on an 'official mission', at least that is what our passports said, and so it was obvious that we would be expected to attend certain official functions and look presentable. Margo came to my rescue and made all my evening and semi-formal wear, but although I was deeply grateful to her, it really was a dreadful bore to me to have to waste my precious time shopping for materials and patterns and then later standing tediously in one position for fittings. Clothes have never been of great importance to me, and it seems an amusing accident that I have somehow always managed to look presentable at the right times.[4] The collecting of the animal equipment was

---

[4] My wife's idea of looking presentable at the right time varies. On the very rare occasions when I can get her to come out, she seems to imagine that the ideal clothing for any occasion, from an Investiture to a cocktail party, consists of faded jeans, a pullover seventeen sizes too large, and a pair of shoes through which her toes peep coyly. I have occasionally, and with much effort, managed to cram her into an evening dress, but the exercise has left me so limp with exhaustion that—now I am getting older—I very rarely attempt it. G.D.

infinitely more fascinating, as far as I was concerned. Gundry's of Bridport made us special nets for catching various creatures, a London manufacturer made us special Humming Bird feeding pots, and all the chemists and animal stores were raided by an army of our friends to produce lamb's teats and feeding bottles; everyone was pressed into service, even into searching their attics for old, long forgotten trunks and boxes to pack everything into. Many a dear friendship fell by the wayside as a result. Our small flat really did look like a junk shop now, and poor Sophie could hardly get in in the mornings, never mind reach her desk which was sandwiched between a couple of large tin trunks. But she never grumbled or fussed, and stoically went on with her typing and tea-making—a new job she had recently acquired.

At this point our family doctor appeared, brandishing a long list of injections that were necessary if we were to set foot on South American soil.

'Surely all these aren't necessary,' I complained.

'Maybe not,' he said, shaking his head, 'but you two have given me enough trouble as it is without staggering back with some foul tropical disease, so whether you like it or not you are going to have smallpox, tetanus, cholera, diphtheria, yellow fever, typhus, typhoid and anything else I can think of, so you had better ring my secretary and make appointments.'

To tell the truth the majority of them were really innocuous but the typhus-typhoid injection must have been developed by sadists to persuade poor, innocent would-be travellers to stay at home for ever, for never have I felt so ghastly. All I got from Durrell, who had been through all this before, of course, was that it was all well worth it and anyway, just think what the actual disease was like if this was the result of a mere injection. This was small comfort to me when my head was bursting and my poor left arm was agonised and useless. Mercifully, these delightful injections came to an end at last, and I honestly think that our doctor was almost sorry that he could think of nothing else to plague us with. It should be a golden rule that one should never befriend a doctor, for he can always retaliate in the most underhand ways.

The main bulk of our luggage was sent on in advance, which helped to clear our room slightly, and give us a little more space in which to pack up our personal belongings. It also enabled us to clear up some of the mess in the flat— or rather it enabled Sophie to do so, for the moment our backs were turned, however briefly, she would rush round the room, clutching brush, pan and Hoover, trying, as she said, 'to make a pathway to my corner'.

'Thank God I'm at least one book ahead now,' sighed Durrell.

Before finishing all the packing I thought it would be wiser to ask our travel agent if we would need to change for dinner on board this passenger ship, for I did not want to put the formal clothes in the baggage room if they would be needed. The man we spoke to assured us most definitely that we would not need any formal clothing.

'Thank God for that,' sighed Durrell. 'I can't bear these floating hotels.'

Literally twenty four hours before we were due to sail, we received a letter from the shipping company enclosing a form for our signature, which stated, quite simply, that as we realised that we were travelling with Spanish and Portuguese immigrants it would be necessary for us to share the public facilities such as toilets, dining-room and saloons with them, but to avoid any repercussions, would we please sign the enclosed document, thus releasing the shipping company from any responsibility. Durrell was furious and rushed to the telephone. The suave voice at the other end assured him that this was quite common practice and that they had sent many people to the Argentine in this way and had never received any complaints. Thus reassured, Durrell signed the form and returned it to the Shipping Officer. Despite this neither of us was particularly thrilled at the prospect.

'It's our own fault,' moaned Durrell, 'we should have

gone to Grindlays' and used their shipping department, as I've always done, instead of trusting somebody strange. Still, it's too late now so we'll just have to make the most of it.'

It was with great sorrow that we said goodbye to Sophie, for she had become an integral part of our small family circle. She too was sorry to have to leave us, and would have liked nothing better than to be coming with us. However, she did assure us that if she was free when we got back she would most certainly come and work for us again.

The whole family turned out to see us off from Bournemouth Central, and in some ways I was quite sorry to leave the town that had been my home for over three years. We joined the boat train at King's Cross Station in London, took a hasty look at our fellow passengers, and were far from impressed by their frozen exteriors. Still, you never know, they might thaw out in the sun.

At Tilbury we were quickly ushered off the train and down a tunnel to the boat where a rather pleasant young officer waited to receive us. Durrell presented our tickets and we were amused to see the young man's reactions to our tourist class tickets.

'Very sorry, sir, not this gangway I'm afraid, but that one aft,' he said, pointing towards the end of the huge ship where a plain wooden gangway led up to the deck. Thanking him, we made our way down the quayside, trying to avoid ropes and bollards, until we eventually reached the gangway he had shown us, but there was not a soul in sight to guide us anywhere. Once on deck we discovered a steward skulking in a doorway out of the rain but, to our alarm, he did not speak a word of English. Undeterred, Durrell waved our tickets under his nose, which seemed to mean something to the man for he beckoned us to follow him. Inside the door we came into a dark and sinister looking saloon with a door at one side and a few pub-like tables and chairs scattered around. At one of these tables sat a small, dark officer, who took our tickets and then obviously told the steward to take us somewhere down the companionway at the right-hand side of the room. No smile of welcome here or, indeed, any interest at all, but the poor man was probably harassed to death. Finally, after wandering through a maze of corridors, we reached our accommodation and were horrified to find that it looked like an overgrown coffin with no portholes and was just large enough to contain the two-tier bunk and a minute table, which left a meagre section of cabin for standing room only.

'This is bloody ridiculous,' Durrell stormed, 'I'm going to see the Chief Steward and get us moved whatever it costs, and when I get back to England I'm going to tear that so-called travel agent off a strip that he won't forget.'

I waited in the 'cabin' while Durrell tore off through the ship to the Purser's Office. The door of the cabin opposite opened and a grey-haired, middle-aged lady stepped out, carrying a Thermos flask. Hopefully I smiled and said 'good afternoon'. She returned my greeting and introduced herself.

'I'm Mrs. Pearce,' she said, 'and my husband and I are going back to Buenos Aires.'

I quickly introduced myself and explained about our shock at the accommodation.

'Yes, I know, dear. It's not too bad coming over as they don't carry immigrants that way, but going back is dreadful. Believe me, we wouldn't be travelling this way if we could afford not to, but my poor husband is on a South American Railways pension and it costs so much more by the better ships. But why on earth are you travelling this way? Didn't your travel agent warn you?'

I explained to her about the dear travel agent and his many assurances about the ship and its accommodation and that there had never been any complaints from any of his clients travelling this way. This made her smile broadly.

'My dear girl, on every trip there are complaints, not so much about the poor immigrants, who don't know any better anyway, but mainly about the cockroaches, the accommodation in the saloon—where they sell only beer, incidentally—and the really dreadful food, but no one appears to take any notice at all. Just you wait until you see how those poor wretched immigrants have to sleep. It's worse than carrying animals and almost like the old slave ships.'[5]

At this juncture Durrell returned, with a long tragic face.

'I'm sorry, Jacquie, but the wretched ship is full and we just can't move from here, though they promised to let me know if they get a cancellation. Really, I could kick myself for being such an idiot and believing that character at the travel agent's.'

Mrs. Pearce was still standing beside me so I apologised to her and introduced Gerry.

'I know it's a great disappointment for you,' she said, 'but there are several Anglo-Argentinians on board and we'll all do our best to make your trip enjoyable. The other consolation is that we do call in at some very interesting places, often staying for a couple of days, so that will relieve the monotony a bit. It's a great pity that you couldn't have got an outside cabin, though, like ours, with a porthole, as it's going to get very hot later; but perhaps someone is getting off before you and then you can change.'

She excused herself and left us to worry about where we were going to put all our luggage in such a tiny space.

'It will all just have to go in the baggage room,' said Durrell.

'But how do we get our clothes out when we need them later on?'

'Let's deal with that problem when it comes, and concentrate on deciding which cases we need now.'

[5] This is nothing but the truth. The way that the immigrants were handled was beyond belief. Short of being actually chained together, the similarity to the old blackbirders was unpleasant, to say the least. I believe that this method of shipping immigrants has now been stopped; for the immigrants' sake, I sincerely hope so. G.D.

After much trouble we accomplished the move, despite our reluctant steward, and then tried to fit ourselves into what space was left.

A few years later I met several ex-Service people who had had the dubious pleasure of travelling in this particular ship during the war, and they all readily sympathised with me when I described the joys of our voyage. The only thing that seemed to surprise them was that the 'hell-ship', as they called it, was still afloat.

'It's probably all those cockroaches that keep it buoyant,' said one of them.

Of the actual voyage out to Buenos Aires I honestly only remember the nice things. All the passengers that we met were absolutely charming, even those whose language we did not know, and there was a hilarious scene in the dining saloon one lunchtime when a very large, homosexual Spanish steward tried making advances to Gerry. Amid much laughter, one of our Spanish-speaking companions endeavoured to explain to this dear individual that, far from being interested in the steward, Gerry happened to be married to me; but the steward simply refused to believe this for, as he pointed out quite forcibly, the señor was not wearing a wedding ring and therefore simply could not be married. After a great deal of persuasion the steward decided that he was pursuing a reluctant relationship. There were also enlivening scenes in the communal lavatories, especially the Ladies', which, because most of the immigrants could not read or write, was normally infested with males who proceeded to remove all the lavatory seats, presumably under the impression that they would make excellent picture frames. Anyway, they were never renewed throughout the whole voyage.

Another delightful habit that our Spanish and Portuguese friends had was to strew the ship's deck with orange peel and anything else that should normally have been consigned to the sea. It was impossible to use the communal bath, as it was never really clean and always looked as though a large grizzly bear had recently bathed in it and lost half his fur in doing so.

Yet despite these minor drawbacks our fellow passengers were great fun and every night they would sing, play guitars and dance and, although none of us could understand each other, we all got on extremely well. Looking back, it was an excellent way to be introduced to the Spanish and Portuguese temperaments and it also enabled us to pick up a few basic Spanish phrases, which proved extremely useful to us once we got out of Buenos Aires. I loved every minute of it but poor Durrell could not get over his acute disappointment at the bad accommodation and dreadful food.

We visited some fascinating places—the fishing port of Vigo in Spain; lovely Lisbon, with its ancient buildings and heavenly blue tiles; the Canary Islands with their itinerant traders and cheap Spanish brandy; Recife in Northern Brazil, full of candied skyscrapers, all with huge cracks down the sides, surrounded by the creeping jungle but full of the most beautiful women; Rio with its tessellated pavements, incessant peevish car horns and weird, sugar-loaf mountain; the coffee port of Santos, gateway to magnificent São Paulo, the largest city in Brazil; down to shabby, friendly Montevideo, graveyard of the *Graf Spee*; then up the muddy Rio de la Plata to the beautiful skyline of Buenos Aires looming through the morning mist, marking the end of Durrell's misery.

During our leave-taking with the Pearces in the corridor just outside our cabins, we were rudely interrupted by a very red-faced junior officer, who was followed closely by an elegantly dressed man who looked exactly like Adolphe Menjou.

'I'm George Gibbs from the British Embassy,' he said by way of introduction, 'and I have been sent down to clear your stuff through the Customs and see you settled in at Mrs. Greenslet's flat.'

He chuckled.

'You know, I had quite a job to find you. Up in first class no one knew you were even on board.'

'That I can well believe,' Gerry replied wryly. 'Nothing below first class appears to interest this ship's personnel. Anyway, I'd rather have this lot as fellow passengers compared with some of the ghastly first class people we've seen at some of the ports of call.'

Gibbs grinned appreciatively.

'Well, now, exactly what have you in the way of luggage, that is, apart from the hold stuff?'

Our respect for Mr. Gibbs rose tremendously when we saw the ease with which all our stuff was cleared through the Customs, while all the other passengers were involved in heated arguments with the white-coated Customs officers. Then we were whisked through the lovely, tree-lined streets of Buenos Aires and installed in Mrs. Greenslet's beautiful flat overlooking the harbour. This very kind lady was a friend of Larry Durrell's and had most unwisely offered to accommodate us on our arrival, which she must have had much cause to regret later. Larry had also given us a long list of people whom it was imperative that we contact on our arrival; by far the most important one was a Señora Bebita Ferreyra.

'You simply must meet this darling woman and give her my undying love. She saved my sanity in the Argentine,' he had said.

With these instructions we could do nothing else. When Gerry telephoned her, she invited us to go to her flat and have lunch. At that time, 1954, the most elusive thing in the Argentine was a taxi, and one soon became inured either to waiting up to half an hour for a free one, or just walking to one's destination. However, we were lucky and got one within fifteen minutes and, in our very halting Spanish, directed him to Calle Posadas. The Ferreyra flat was to become a haven for us during our eight months in South America, and Bebita our Guardian Angel, who could literally perform miracles. She could organise anything ranging from housing a collection of animals to persuading an irate Buenos Aires taxi driver to take six Black-Necked Swans in his car. There was nothing that she could not accomplish, always insisting that everyone was adorable, angelic and sweet, and they really were— for her.

The flat was a most charming apartment, cool and peaceful, and Señora Ferreyra apparently catered for everyone's taste, for the tables were covered with publications dealing with modern art, literature, music, ballet; a grand piano dominated one small drawing-room and music was scattered about on the top of it. But the one thing that really riveted our attention as we came in was a large portrait on one of the walls of a strikingly beautiful woman seated before a piano and wearing a large brown picture hat.

'Surely to heaven that's not her,' I said.

'Probably,' said Gerry, 'but she certainly won't look like that now.'

At that moment Señora Ferreyra chose to enter the room, looking far lovelier than her portrait.

'I am B-b-bebita Ferreyra, how lovely to see you both. Larry told me a lot about you, Gerry, when he was here with the British Council.'

'We're sorry to intrude upon you like this,' Gerry replied, 'but Larry positively insisted that we did.'

'B-b-b-but naturally you must. I would have been very insulted if you had not. How is that angel Larry?'

'He sends you his undying love and hopes you will come to Europe very soon.'

'Come, children, we must go and eat, and you are both to come here as often as you like and if I can help you at all I will.'

Our original plan had been to include Chile in the itinerary in the hope of collecting some wildfowl for Peter Scott's place at Slimbridge, but here again our helpful travel agent had not thought to tell us that this time of the year was the height of the holiday season and plane reservations were impossible to get. Durrell was livid and that evening poured out his soul to Bebita.

'Where else would you like to go then, Gerry?'

'Well, it's rather difficult at this juncture but I think Paraguay might be interesting and I would love to try and catch a giant armadillo.'

'Perhaps something can be arranged,' smiled Bebita. 'I will speak to my brother, Boy, tomorrow and I will telephone you.'

In the meantime we received an invitation through a friend of Gerry's, Ian Gibson, to stay on his cousin's *estancia* a few miles away from Buenos Aires along the coast road. 'Los Ingleses' was an enchanting place, very old and apparently the place where the great naturalist W. H. Hudson had stayed and prepared his notes for his famous work on the birds of La Plata. The Boote family were charming and welcomed us with great warmth and were soon deeply involved in *bicho* hunting. I was very fortunate to have my first real introduction to the Argentine pampas through these delightful people, and it accounts, in no small measure, for my great love of that country. The *estancia* spread for miles and the vast areas of grassland were interspersed with small lagoons surrounded by the silver pampas grass and small knots of trees or *monte*. The grounds surrounding the house had been well planted with poplars, eucalyptus and pine trees, which rustled in the slight breeze which always seems an essential part of the Argentine scene. The house itself was a low, Spanish style *hacienda* with flag floors and oil lamps. The furnishings were simple and our bedroom contained a very large goose-feather bed, a small chest of drawers, a couple of chairs and a dressing table.

During the long week-end that we stayed there, we soon got together a weird assortment of the various wild creatures that live in the surrounding country, ranging from armadillos to a baby screamer bird whom we called Eggbert. He looked like a badly made child's fluffy toy, covered with egg-coloured fluff from his domed head right down to his bright red legs. He had bright, boot-button eyes and a long, inquisitive beak, and a pair of the most enormous feet that I had ever seen on any baby animal, over which he seemed to have absolutely no control. As he staggered around the garden, these feet seemed to take complete control of their unfortunate owner, who bleeped plaintively when he found himself in a tangled mess as a result. We were all in love with Eggbert but he was a terrible problem to us, for nothing we offered him to eat was to his liking. Elizabeth, one of the daughters, suggested that we give Eggbert the freedom of the vegetable garden for, as she wisely argued, the bird would probably have enough sense to show us which of the many varieties of vegetables he liked. Eggbert manfully staggered down each row, stopping occasionally to peck at carrots, onions, cabbages, but as he came to the spinach he stopped, squawked, and waddled into the middle of it.

'Victory!' shouted Durrell, but Eggbert was still not having any.

'You know,' I said, 'it's quite obvious even to a dimwit like me that if baby screamers are usually fed on regurgitated matter that their mums and dads provide for them, that's what we ought to do. You tell me that screamers eat alfalfa. Well, surely, when it comes up from the mum's gullet, it's all wet and sticky; so why don't we chew a bit of this spinach and see if he likes it that way?'

'Jolly good idea,' said Durrell, 'but who is going to do the chewing? I'm afraid I can't.'

'Why not?' I asked.

'I smoke and nicotine might upset the poor little fellow very badly.'

'All right,' I said, 'I'll have a go.'

I've never been particularly fond of spinach, and since that glorious week-end I have not been able to face it in any shape or form. The only consolation I could get for my aching jaw was that Eggbert liked it very much indeed and flourished remarkably.

Reluctantly we left 'Los Ingleses' and the Bootes and

carried our mixed assortment of creatures back to the capital.

'There is just one small problem, Gerry dear, where do we keep all these creatures until we can send them off by air?'

'Oh, don't worry about that, I'll just ask Mr. Gibbs at the Embassy, and if he can't help I'll try somebody else.'[6]

Poor George Gibbs was absolutely shattered on being asked over the telephone to find shelter for wild animals, although, to do the man credit, he did ask several of his friends to help. Suddenly it came to me. Who else could help us but Bebita?

'Leave it to me, child, and I will telephone you in half an hour. Come and have dinner tonight anyway but don't worry, I'll find you somewhere,' she said when we phoned her.

Half an hour later, she rang back.

'I have found you a place, my children, it is a friend's house and you can keep your animals in his garage. Here is the address.'

The 'house' proved to be a large and luxurious mansion in the Buenos Aires equivalent of Park Lane, but at least it solved our problem and was the talking point at the British Embassy for days afterwards, for the 'friend' was apparently one of the richest men in the Argentine and had, as I suspected, been brow-beaten by Bebita into accepting us and our brood.

During dinner later that evening, Bebita told us that she had another friend who had offered to let us visit his property in Paraguay.

'It is quite simple; you fly to Asunción, then his private plane will take you to Puerto Casado, his large estate, and

[6] I can see nothing laughable in my contention that a British Embassy is created in any out-of-the-way part of the world in order to help the visiting animal collector. The fact that, in my experience, the average Embassy does not share my belief just goes to show why I feel our whole foreign policy ought to be overhauled and reviewed. G.D.

you can stay there and collect all your beloved animals. Would you like this, Gerry?'

Needless to say, we were overwhelmed by it all but suddenly remembered our rather dog-Spanish.

'Bebita, my love, much as we would love to go to your friend's estate, how can we do without someone to translate for us?'

'That is no problem either, children. You remember Rafael Soto, my painter friend's youngest son? Well, he is on holiday from school; I have discussed it with his mother and she is delighted, so everything is settled. Now eat your dinner.'

So it was that a few days later we flew with Rafael up to Asunción and the tremendous humid heat, exchanging the vast open grasslands of Argentina for the swampy cactus region and the vistas of Paraguay. In doing so the three of us shared the doubtful pleasure of flying in a single-engined aircraft over the Matto Grosso with an over-enthusiastic Brazilian pilot. However, we soon became engrossed in the landscape below us, with the peculiar flat-topped mountains in the distance, and Conan Doyle's 'Lost World' seemed a very real thing.

'I'd hate to have to come down in that,' said Gerry. 'No one would ever find you.'

When we eventually landed on the tiny airfield, we were greeted by a rather surly individual who turned out to be the manager of the estate and who looked anything but overjoyed to see us. But he had his orders to house and feed us and offer us all the necessary assistance, although how he interpreted these orders was, unfortunately, left entirely to him. Soon we were all installed in a somewhat ramshackle bungalow in the small village which surrounded the tannin factory—the reason for the existence of Puerto Casado. A vast housekeeper, Paula, was there to greet us. Much to Rafael's amusement, he soon found out that she was the local 'Madame' and, by virtue of this, was perhaps the most important person in the entire village.

'This is an advantage, Gerry,' Rafael said. 'If we wish anything to be done we ask Paula.'

Rafael proved invaluable and soon had the entire place organised. There was only one method of travelling any distance in this area and that was by the strange, narrow-gauge railway which traversed the swamps. The actual vehicles used were oddly shaped carriages with a Ford V8 engine. These contraptions were mounted on railway wheels and swayed perilously from side to side as they clanked over the buckled rails linking each timber station with the main tannin factory in Casado itself. It was quite obvious that we would get nothing out of the poor, dejected looking Indians who lived in Casado and so the best thing we could do was travel to the very end of the railway line and alert all the stations, setting traps in the most likely places. One *bicho* that we could well have done without and which was forever with us was the mosquito, a large, zebra-striped job which settled on us, whenever we were foolish enough to stop, in absolute swarms. There was nothing that we could do to prevent ourselves from being bitten on every part of our anatomy. They could even penetrate the thick twill of our trousers and as quickly as we killed them, they would be replaced by the same number again. As I was crushing endless handfuls of these nauseating things, I vividly remembered the amused expression of our pilot when he collected us at Asunción and his calm assurance that I would be waiting for him within a week to return to the capital. In face of the mosquitoes, I must admit that I was sorely tempted to take him up on his offer but, like everything else, we soon got used to these constant companions.

The countryside was quite unreal and was a crazy mixture of swamp, cacti of all descriptions, palms and a strange tree with a swollen trunk.

'What on earth's that tree called, Rafael?' I asked.

'Dat it's, how you call *palo borache*, in English, este drunken stick.'

'They're quite fantastic. They're all lounging about just like a Government House cocktail party,' said Gerry.

All the Indians we met were very shy and I was appalled at the conditions under which they were forced to live. Through Rafael I found out that they were paid very little for the very hard work that they did and that their 'houses', which were little more than thrown-together tin shacks, were provided by the generous Company. Their pay was meagre and the poor wretches seemed, like most South American Indians who participated in the benefits of civilisation, to spend most of their money on seeking oblivion by drinking fire-water called *cana*. I was revolted to find that on pay day the Company dispensed their money at one end of the train caravan and sold *cana* to them at the other, instead of encouraging them to buy decent food and clothing for themselves and their children.

Rafael and I discussed the plight of the Indians at length. Although he sympathised with me deeply, he assured me that Paraguayans despised the Indians, whom they considered lower than the oxen who worked on the estates —mainly, I gathered, because they were not 'Christians', whatever that meant. The Paraguayans are the only people I have ever met who would much rather kill an animal in front of you than bargain for a purchase price, and it is my own personal belief that Paraguayans don't even like themselves! I longed to return to the Argentine, and Rafael himself was at times staggered by their behaviour, saying constantly, 'These peoples, they are not nice.'

Our collection of animals, which was housed in a former chicken run, was growing rapidly and soon we were looking after all sorts of lovely things. I naturally had my favourites. Cai, a douracouli monkey that we had purchased from a local Indian woman was one. I was particularly delighted that we had got hold of a douracouli. It is the only nocturnal monkey in the world, but apart from this she was extremely attractive. About the size of a small cat, her fur was a silver grey, but her chest was covered with pale orange down, fading to cream. The eyes were owl-like, pale amber and surrounded with white fur edged in black, and the ears were almost invisible, but the thing

that really was charming was her permanent smile which,
I regret to say, often belies the douracouli's rather unsteady
temperament, although Cai, throughout the time we had
her, was always tame and an admirable companion.

We also had four enchanting guira cuckoos who were the
silliest, most endearing birds who spent their whole day
either peering out of the cleaning gap at the bottom of
their cages to see what was going on, shrilling hysterically
at each other, or looking like badly made feather dusters
when they sunbathed with wings drooped. They are about
the size of an English starling but have a pale fawny cream
plumage streaked with greyish black, tattered gingery crests
on their heads, and long tails like a magpie. The fantastic
thing about them is that they are tame from the moment
you get them. Like magpies they are extremely inquisitive
birds and like nothing better than to peck in your ear or
dig in your scalp, but they are equally at home sitting on
your wrist raising their crests and shrilling madly at one
another. I must admit that I conceived a tremendous liking
for these ridiculous birds. They love to have their heads
scratched, which seemed to induce a trance-like state in
them. Then there was Foxy, a grey fox who would eat
cigarette ends with disastrous results to his innards; Pooh,
a crab-eating racoon who had an insatiable appetite for
anything that his vast, twitching paws could pull into his
orbit; and finally Sarah Huggersack, a baby giant anteater
who had to be bottle-fed and whose idea of ecstasy was to
cling, with razor-like claws, either to Gerry or me, or
better still, to a straw-filled sack. Gerry simply adored her
and she him, and he fussed over her feeding like a father
with his first-born. Nothing was too good for her or too
much trouble, and she soon realised it. She shared his bed
at night ('she mustn't catch cold') and his every free
moment ('it is essential that she feels loved; after all she
would normally be clinging to her mother all day'). I got
scant attention those days[7] so I contented myself with

[7] I think this remark is slightly unkind. There was nothing to prevent Jacquie sharing a bed with both me and Sarah. G.D.

looking after the other animals and was soon rewarded by their trust and affection.

Apart from looking after the animals we were making our first film for television and also trying to cope with the various idiosyncrasies of the things and people around us. On the whole I felt very pleased with myself; I had adjusted fairly well to my surroundings, and even Durrell was pleased with my animal work. I had a natural flair for it, he said, and he assured me that he meant it sincerely. He rarely gave praise when it came to such a serious matter as animal care. Nevertheless, he teased me unmercifully about my fright over finding a vampire bat sharing our lavatory, although I soon got used to the little creature flying out past my head whenever I entered. He was also unsympathetic about my reluctance to share my bed with such things as orange armadillos, baby coatis and anything else the Indians saw fit to bring to our bungalow.

'I don't care who you share your bed with, Durrell, but I'm fussy,' I said determinedly.

This was greeted with shouts of laughter by both Rafael and Durrell, but it did not stop Gerry from presenting me with a vast assortment of animals to take into my bed, and there is nothing quite like having your mattress sodden with copious floods of animal urine; it makes all the world kin!

As it got near the time for us to leave Paraguay, Durrell was still fretting and fussing that we had not got hold of the Maned Wolf, and he simply could not understand why, for apparently the place was swarming with them, although we never saw any in our travels. Until one afternoon Rafael burst into the bungalow, full of some gossip that he had overheard. Apparently an Indian a few kilometres up the line had caught one of these beautiful animals in a trap and had, as promised, told the office in Casado, but no one had thought to pass on the message to us. Durrell was beside himself with rage and worry.

'If we don't get that animal soon it will die. They're damned delicate creatures. Where is it, Rafael?'

'Don't worry, Gerry, I have arranged to bring it to you today,' promised Rafael.

Poor Durrell could not contain himself and kept dashing over to the railhead to see if anything was happening. Shortly before five o'clock the 'train' arrived and Rafael and Gerry carefully lifted the cage off and brought it into the chicken run enclosure. The poor animal was completely exhausted and very thin and, to my eyes, looked near to death.

'How long has the Indian had this, Rafael?'

'Truly, Gerry, I do not know, but it must be many days as the animal is not well.'

It really was a lovely thing, with long, slender legs like a deer, long pointed ears and bright red fur.

'I think the animal has pneumonia,' said Gerry. 'Let's try and get him into a bigger cage and get some food into him.'

This we did, very carefully, but the animal was so weak that he made no attempt to bite or stop us touching him.

'It's bloody criminal that this animal should have been left to get into this state through inefficiency. If I ever find out who was to blame, I'll do something desperate to him.'

'Look, Gerry,' I said, 'I know how you feel, but things do happen even in well-organised offices and all we can do now is try to get the animal well again.'

It was almost as though the wolf realised that we were trying to help him, and he did lap up the milk and raw eggs and glucose. Then we tried finely minced meat and liver, all of which he ate, but despite this I think we all realised that it was hopeless. The pneumonia was well advanced by the time he had got to us and despite our constant nursing and feeding, nothing we could do could have saved him. Gerry was heart-broken and insisted on doing a post mortem. This revealed the pneumonia but also showed internal injuries, as though the animal had had a severe blow.

This episode subdued all three of us for the next twenty-four hours, then suddenly something happened to take our minds completely off the whole thing. A revolution broke out in Asunción. To begin with we all roared with laughter for, as everyone knows, revolutions are—after football—the favourite occupation of the South Americans. But then we received a radio message from a charming American who lived farther up the river. He knew that we planned to leave and transport the entire collection down to Buenos Aires by river, and he was very concerned when he heard that all the river traffic had been commandeered. He suggested to us that we make use of his four-seater plane. This was fine, except for one thing—what would we do with all our animals? We could not stay in Paraguay any longer for we had to get back to Buenos Aires to catch our ship back to London. To me there was only one solution : to let the main bulk of the collection go and take what we could in the plane. For two whole days Gerry wrestled with this problem. He was worried that the majority of these creatures might no longer be able to fend for themselves. But finally he admitted that it was the only thing to do. Foxy we gave to Paula, who adored him, and apart from our favourites, who were all babies, we opened the cages and offered the rest their freedom. To our intense astonishment none of them appeared to want to go and several of them hung around for days, waiting to be fed. But Gerry warned us not to feed them.

'They will only go on hanging about if you do, and the locals might shoot them then. They'll all go away eventually, when they learn that their regular meals are not going to be provided.'

'So much for all that sentimental twaddle that I was reared on that all God's creatures need to be free,' I exploded.

'Remember, I told you in Manchester that animals take to captivity quite readily if treated properly, but you never really believed me.'

'No, I didn't, but I am utterly convinced now.'

Then there was a brief lull in the fighting while the two sides talked. Our American friend urged us to leave while we could as air services to Buenos Aires were apparently being resumed during this brief respite. His plane flew into Casado that afternoon and we pushed ourselves and our animals into the tiny cockpit. The pilot looked doubtful, but nevertheless taxied off. After three attempts, we made it into the air.

'Well, we got away,' he observed. 'Let's hope we can get down,' and with this we made for the capital.

Our landing was a nightmare, especially as the field of the aero-club was waterlogged after the recent heavy rains. As our wheels touched the ground the ship began to lurch madly from side to side, making noises rather like a distressed destroyer, and I began to think that we were going to turn right over. However, she finally corrected herself and came to a halt.

'So sorry about that,' the pilot smiled, 'but we were a little overweight; not a good thing for a light plane. Still, we got here.'

Thankfully we climbed down and dashed across the city to the commercial airport, just in time to be bundled into a Branif flight to Buenos Aires.

'Thank God we made it,' Gerry breathed, 'though there were moments back there when I thought we never would.'

Eventually the lights of Buenos Aires twinkled below us and we touched down, to find Mr. Gibbs once more in attendance.

As we walked across to the airport buildings we briefly outlined what had happened.

'By the way, there's a slight difficulty about these animals of yours. Have you got a health permit for them?'

'Now where on earth would I get that from, with a revolution going on?' Durrell asked.

'That's what I told them all, but you know what the official mind is like. Still, come and talk to the government vet, he seems a decent chap.'

He was, after a great deal of persuasion from Gerry.

Bebita was delighted to see us and, of course, had arranged for us to put the animals in Rafael's grandmother's house overnight and then move them next day to a friend's house in Belgrano, a suburb of Buenos Aires.

We added a few things to our nucleus by going with Rafael to his family's *estancia* just outside the capital and buying from the animal dealers in the city itself. I became a dab hand at cage construction and at shopping in Spanish, helping to get permits and establishing all our animals to face the three-week voyage which lay ahead.

After a final exhausting day dealing with the Argentine Customs and showing everyone on the dockside our papers, we at last found ourselves at the rail of the Blue Star ship, waving goodbye to all our many dear friends. I was deeply sorry to have to leave that lovely country and I promised myself that we would be back, and that this time nothing would induce me to leave Argentina for another country.

On the forward deck our charges settled down for the night under the heavy tarpaulin which the ship had provided, and we went to bed early, for we had a lot to do the next day, sorting the cages out and feeding the animals as soon as it was light. Before we left them for the night, though, Sarah had her bottle and a loving hug from Gerry.

'She is a dear little thing,' he said, and added mournfully, 'I do wish we could have her in our cabin.'

CHAPTER 4

Bringing a collection of animals back by sea was another new experience for me, and the thought of it had terrified me, for not only was I a very bad sailor, but I was certain that the constant anxiety on the animals' behalf would ruin any pleasure that the voyage itself might hold. Strangely enough, though, I just did not have time to feel sick or even worry about it, because right from the first day on board we were kept so busy. We soon developed a regular routine: at first light, with the aid of a cup of tea, we would stagger down on to the forward deck and start the business of cleaning out cages and washing feeding pots. While all this is not too bad when the sea is calm and the weather warm, it becomes progressively less pleasant the nearer one gets to the northern European waters and their usual icy blasts. The Captain and crew of the *Paraguay Star* had done everything they could to make our animals comfortable, and having only a small collection, it was fairly easy to house them in a simple structure which the 'Chippy' erected from planks and old tarpaulins. On our voyage up the Brazilian coast we could spray all the birds regularly (in lieu of a bath) without having to worry about their catching cold. Sarah had a wonderful time for she was allowed, three times a day, to run all the way round the deck, honking vigorously, in pursuit of Durrell's legs. The young officers were always eager to help us and one of them incurred the Master's wrath by turning up late for a watch as a result of carrying buckets of water for us. No passengers were allowed on the forward deck, as this was cargo space, and it was amusing to look up and see hordes of faces pressed to the glass bulkheads watching us. Our exclusiveness made us unpopular with the majority of the older passengers, all well seasoned South American coasters, but we struck up a very close friendship with about half a dozen other people in our own age group and, as a result, had quite a lot of fun, especially at the fancy-dress ball where Gerry and I, dressed as Paraguayans, ran off with the first prize, to the chagrin of the other competitors. The riotous party that was held in our friends' cabin later that night caused the Captain's fury to descend on a few more of the younger officers.

Cleaning out large lumps of excreta when you are suffering from a severe hangover and a queasy stomach is not to be recommended, especially at sea. How on earth I ever got through the following morning without having to lean over the rails, I shall never know.

At the various ports of call, the First Officer very sweetly arranged for a permanent watch to be maintained, to enable us to go ashore and get any fresh food supplies that we needed, and I am sure that there was only one person in the entire ship's company who was delighted and relieved when we eventually tied up at Victoria Dock, London—the ship's Master.

Most of our tiny collection found its way to Paignton Zoo, where Sarah quite readily accepted the love and attention of someone else, although she never completely forgot her darling foster father. It was heart-breaking, in many ways, to part with all these lovely creatures, and I began to realise how Durrell must have felt on his previous trips and why he had this burning ambition to have a zoo of his own, so he would not be forced to part with the animals that he brought back.

Our arrival in Bournemouth soon reached Sophie's ears. She, in the meantime, had got a job working for a local builder, and although she found the work interesting, we had no difficulty whatsoever in persuading her to leave and return to the fold.

To Gerry's annoyance Hart-Davis had, in our absence, decided to publish *The Bafut Beagles*. This was a blow, as he had anticipated being a book in hand and instead found the proofs of the African book waiting for him.

'I do hope they're not going to do this every time I catch up with myself,' he wailed, 'otherwise I shall go mad. I suppose I'd better start on the one about this trip before you all start nagging me.'

Thus was *The Drunken Forest* begun but, I regret to say, not always assiduously pursued, at least not without a lot of badgering from either Sophie or me.

'Why can't you two hags realise that I am not a machine? I can't just turn it on like a tap when I want to. I only wish I could. I have to wait for inspiration. You two are getting like those awful people who keep telling me that it's so easy to write a book and that they could do it themselves if only they had the time. Well, all I can suggest is that you all try it some time !'

But in spite of all the arguments and black looks, it was

eventually finished and I do not know which of us was more relieved. Durrell's reluctance to write up this particular trip was understandable for, after all, it had been somewhat of a failure, but Spencer Curtis Brown reassured us:

'People love to read about failures, you know, Gerry. It makes them feel that writers are human after all. If it's even a partial success then it's interesting.'

We were all further encouraged by the news that *The Bafut Beagles* had been chosen by World Books, and to celebrate this event Spencer threw a lavish dinner party for us at the Savoy Hotel. Flushed with enthusiasm Durrell, in a weak moment, allowed himself to be persuaded into writing a children's book for Collins, to be based on the three areas of the world covered by *The Overloaded Ark*, *Three Singles* and *The Drunken Forest*. Although it seemed a very good idea at the time, never have Sophie and I suffered so much in the cause of literature. For some unknown reason Durrell just did not want to finish this book, and in sheer desperation Sophie and I set about writing the final chapter. This was naturally tossed aside with scorn by the genius when we had completed it, but it did inspire him to re-write it and get the thing out of the way.

'Gerry, darling,' I asked him one day, 'why don't you have a system as Larry does? He writes 2,000 words every morning and then the rest of the day he can devote to other things.'

Durrell groaned.

'Believe me, I only wish I could, but the subtle difference between us is that he loves writing and I don't. To me it's simply a way to make money which enables me to do my animal work, nothing more. I'm not a serious writer in that sense, but merely a hack journalist who has the good fortune to be able to sell what he writes.'

It was perhaps a good thing, since we were all getting on one another's nerves, that we received an invitation from Brother Larry, who was now Director of Information in Cyprus, to go and visit him. Knowing of Gerry's fascination with films and film-making, Larry also suggested that he might get to know the island by making a film about it. Gerry needed no excuse for leaving 'Pudding Island', and soon we were once again surrounded by odd bits of equipment.

However, before we left, Gerry was asked to give an illustrated lecture at London's Festival Hall. The idea terrified him, but as Hart-Davis thought it was good publicity for his books, he eventually agreed. The entire family bore the strain and worry of this venture, for we all knew how much Gerry loathed public appearances and, although he is an excellent lecturer and amuses every audience with his lightning charcoal sketches of the animals he is talking about, he is deeply convinced that he is no lecturer. As it had been decided that there ought to be an animal for Gerry to introduce at the end of his talk, we asked Paignton Zoo if they could lend us Sarah Huggersack.

On the great day we all presented ourselves at the Festival Hall. Sarah, who had arrived before us, was ensconced in the dressing-room just vacated by Sir Thomas Beecham, while we poor mortals were left to fend for ourselves. As we expected, the lecture was a tremendous success but it was Sarah Huggersack who stole the show, running along the stage, playing with Gerry and honking madly. She accepted completely the adulation that was showered upon her from all sides and became so excited that she did not want to get back into her travelling box. That she loved the limelight was again underlined a little later when she appeared in her first television programme and captivated even the stoniest-hearted stage-hand at the Television Centre. But, like most great stars, Sarah developed a temperament—being a star, she needed to be appreciated.

Our trip to Cyprus was marred from the very beginning, and during the cocktail party that Larry gave to introduce us to Cypriot society, the first bomb was exploded. It seemed that our arrival in the island was the last provocation that the Cypriots needed to show their disapproval

of the British in general. In view of the terrorist activities
we naturally had to give up the idea of travelling round
the island in a government film van, camping out. However,
there was an alternative; we established ourselves in Larry's
house in the picturesque village of Bellapaise, just north of
Kyrenia, and Gerry began to start work on a documentary
film designed to show the importance of a water supply to
a Cypriot village. We were all adopted into the life of the
village, for not only was Larry himself popular, and respected by the villagers, but Gerry, thanks to his childhood
spent in Corfu, could speak enough Greek and remember
enough Greek songs to make him accepted. We became
particularly friendly with the mayor, who took us all over
the island, even into the so-called strongholds of the Eoka
terrorists and, despite the stories we heard of anti-British
feeling, we never at any time were either molested or shown
any ill-feeling during our stay in the island. We were very
saddened to feel that lack of understanding had destroyed
the remarkable relationship which had existed in the island
for so long—a feeling that Larry later expressed so well in
his book *Bitter Lemons*.

We finally had to leave Cyprus unexpectedly because of
some television negotiations which had come to a head.
Some friends offered us the use of their flat just outside
London for two weeks, while they were away, and at
this point Durrell chose to go down with jaundice. Like
many other people, I had always looked upon this com-
plaint as rather a joke, something music-hall comedians
often referred to, so it was a little shattering to be told by
the doctor that it was, in fact, quite serious and could be
fatal if certain precautions over diet were not taken. For
two whole weeks I struggled manfully to produce meals
which would tempt a flagging appetite, but I never realised
until then what a strain a non-fat diet could put upon a
marriage, especially when one partner could quite freely
eat such ordinary things as butter, eggs, cheese, milk, cream
and all those delicious things that make life bearable, while

the other was stuck with a diet of steamed fish, grilled meat without butter, dry bread and no alcohol.[1]

After the fortnight was up, Sister Margaret drove up to London to convey a rather seedy Durrell back to the bosom of his family in Bournemouth. There, Durrell's enforced inactivity brought on a sudden urge to write one book that he had been talking about for years. In 1935 the entire Durrell family had moved, *en masse*, to the unsuspecting Greek island of Corfu where they had spent five idyllic years, terminated only by the outbreak of war. It was obvious, from the way they spoke about it, that this period was one of enchantment for the entire family, and Mrs. Durrell had often assured me that it was the only time in her life that she had never had an overdraft. Never have I known Gerry work as he did then; it seemed to pour out of him and it was all that poor Sophie could do to keep pace with his output. Six weeks and 120,000 words later, Durrell collapsed gracefully. It was finished—and so, nearly, was he.

My Family and Other Animals was an overwhelming success, as none of us ever doubted it would be. It had everything that a best seller should have—an exotic island, a crazy family and lots of animals. It breathed sunshine and freedom, and even the critics loved it. Ten years later, this book continues to outsell all the other books, and although it has made us many friends all over the world, it has unfortunately turned Corfu into a tourist attraction —a marvellous thing for the Corfiots and the Greek economy, but a very sad thing for the Durrells, who loved it as it was. The biggest laugh the family have ever had was when they learnt that this particular book had been chosen as one of the set English books for G.C.E. Literature. Durrell had never had any formal schooling but had been tutored by an endless series of eccentric individuals who

[1] You don't mind the steamed fish, grilled meat and dry bread, but in such circumstances to be deprived of alcohol is something which no sane person will put up with. G.D.

had taught him everything but the basic 'three Rs'. However, he gets many letters from grateful sufferers, saying that at least the English Literature exam is a pleasure, even if nothing else is.

Because of all the effort needed to produce *My Family*, poor Durrell was at a very low ebb and was ordered away to the Scilly Isles for a complete rest. Although Gerry knew these lovely islands quite well, I had never been there before and we spent two quiet, windswept weeks walking all over them, staring into rock pools, bird watching and drinking home-made parsnip wine with a lady ornithologist we met.

Now completely cured, Gerry started to think about another trip, but this time he intended to concentrate even more on the filming side. So he purchased a rather expensive German cine-camera and for weeks we were all enveloped in reels of under-exposed cine film while Durrell got his eye in. After a great deal of thought, Gerry decided that the best place to make a good film about a collecting trip was the Cameroons, and in particular the kingdom of his old friend and drinking companion, the Fon of Bafut. He had been there twice before, and argued that when embarking on as involved a project as filming, it was essential to go to an area that he knew well, whose people he got on with and, what was more important, whose animals he could rely on.

As this was obviously going to be a rather bigger operation than usual, I suggested that we took Sophie with us— if she wanted to come. She needed no second invitation. Another thing we decided to do was to approach various manufacturers and ask for their support, not financially but in supplying us with basic essentials in return for the publicity that we could obviously give them. A basic letter was evolved, and in spite of Sophie's tendency to refer to Gerald Durrell's numerous T.B. appearances and to assure the recipient that one of the objects of this trip was to gather material for a new booze,[2] the response was overwhelming.

[2] During this era she also wrote to a manufacturer of toilet goods

The British Railways delivery man and the postman were sick of delivering vast parcels to us, but we never tired of opening them and gasping at the assortment of goods they contained. There was everything from plastic bowls and buckets to carpentry tools, drugs for the animals and for us, elegant nylon shirts and socks, boots, camp beds, tea bags, wire netting, an outboard canoe, an electric generator —in fact we had enough stuff to equip a small army. The other occupants of the house got bored with finding the main entrance constantly blocked by somebody's behind bending over a crate, or by bits of wire left lying around, and it was all that poor Margaret could do to pacify her irate tenants. When it was eventually all assembled it took two large trucks to transport it to Southampton and the waiting banana boat.

By now another person had joined our party. For the first time we had decided to accept one of the many offers of help that we received from would-be animal collectors. We had chosen this particular young man as he was very keen on reptiles and the Cameroons was an excellent area for finding bizarre species. As it was near Christmas Sophie asked if she could join us later as she wanted to spend Christmas with her family and, apart from the Captain and the crew, we three had the entire ship to ourselves. The voyage out was delightful, for it was rather like having one's own private yacht.

Africa as a continent has never appealed to me, certainly never 'called' in the way that it did to Livingstone, but ten days later I was standing on the quayside at Victoria, the main town in the British Cameroons, watching all our luggage being unloaded from a lighter and then transferred to two Bedford trucks, or Mammy wagons as they are called in West Africa. Our journey to Bafut would be done in two stages, with a brief stop at Mamfe, Gerry's old

---

asking for both disinfectant and toilet paper and assuring them that, among many other things, we would furnish them with photographs of their products being used in the field. G.D.

camping site on the banks of the Cross River. We had our
usual contretemps with the local Customs who, for some
reason best known to themselves, wanted to impound our
aluminium Dexion cage (which looked like a giant Meccano
set) with which the firm had so generously supplied us. We
made such a fuss that they eventually agreed to release it,
to the extreme fury of the head of the Customs, a man who
rejoiced in the name of Pine Coffin. We got into trouble
with the Customs again when we reached Mamfe for what
was termed the 'illegal possession' of a revolver, a forbidden
item in West Africa without special permission from the
Governor of Nigeria himself. Unfortunately for them we
had this permission.

Our journey up-country was quite uneventful except for
swirling red dust and rutted roads, which seem an inevitable
part of the African scene under British protection. It has
always been a source of amazement to me that the French
and Belgians could construct reasonable highways in the
territories they controlled, whereas the most the Empire
builders could ever achieve was a meagre strip of macadam
at the outskirts of the principal towns. However, it all adds
to the joys of travel, for there is nothing better than a
twisted back and an aching head to encourage you to stay.

Our first stop was at a small village called Bekebe, a place
that Gerry had stayed in on his other visits, and one of his
former animal boys, Ben, came rushing forward, asking
for employment and presenting us with our very first 'beef'
—a baby black-footed mongoose whom we promptly
christened Tiki, and whom Gerry popped inside his shirt
as we had no boxes available. Having made sure that Ben
was safely in the back with all the other boys—we had
collected a full staff in Victoria with the help of Gerry's
old steward, Pious—we set off again, finally arriving at the
Mamfe U.A.C. Manager's house at about nine o'clock. We
waited in the trucks while Gerry disappeared into the very
elegant looking modern bungalow. He soon reappeared
with the Manager, John Henderson. He was a charming
and amusing host, and during the six weeks that we

infested his house with both ourselves and our 'bloody animals', as he called them, nothing was too much trouble for either him or his staff. He readily admitted that he could not stand our animals, but since he liked us, he would tolerate the rest.

Mamfe is a very small community perched right on the banks of the Cross River, and although delightful for a brief stop, it had nothing to endear itself to me. The climate was revolting—hot and humid both day and night —as a result of which both Sophie and I were covered with sweat rash in spite of constantly bathing and anointing ourselves with various proprietary products which assured us they would cure or prevent this irritating affliction. There were about ten other Europeans on the station, all friendly and helpful, and they promised to 'spread the gospel' to the effect that we were demented Europeans wanting animals. Slowly the veranda around John's house began to look like a pet shop.

'You know, I often think I'm at the wrong house when I see all those bloody animals outside,' bleated John, 'and I nearly drove away this afternoon.'

'Look, John,' said Gerry worriedly, 'if you really dislike them so much we'll move out.'

'Don't be a fool, old boy, only joking, glad to have both you and them.'

Durrell wanted to renew his acquaintance with his hunters so we prepared for initiations into the delights of walking through the tropical forest to visit the remote village where they lived. At dawn, we set off across the river in dug-out canoes, accompanied by rucksacks containing sandwiches and Thermoses full of cold water. On entering the forest on the other side, we walked along a well-defined track at a fairly steady pace in single file. The first things that struck me was the silence of it all and then the heat, which was oppressive. We occasionally heard birds and animals but never saw a thing. So much for the wicked tropical forest, teeming with wild animals and deadly snakes.

After about two exhausting hours we came to a clearing in the forest where we met two lean, elderly natives, leaning on their long sticks.

'Iseeya, Bo,' said Gerry, by way of greeting.

'Welcome, Massa,' they replied in unison, then went off into a stream of pidgin English which completely eluded me, though Gerry fortunately seemed able to understand it. Eventually he gave them cigarettes and waved them good-bye.

'What on earth was all that about?' I asked.

'Oh, nothing, just passing the time of day,' and with that we resumed our march.

At about midday we reached the village of Eshobi, where the bush telegraph had evidently warned the villagers to expect us, for they were all gathered in the main 'street' to welcome us. That they were delighted to see Gerry again was obvious. With beaming smiles and clicking fingers, they chanted, 'Welcom, welcom,' and we were all presented with large, newly collected coconuts; and, believe me, after several hours' walk through a hot African forest, there is nothing more refreshing than the juice of a coconut. Two very rickety chairs were produced for us to sit on and I sank down gratefully, hot and sweaty after so much exertion, and had a good look at the village itself. Compared with the other villages that we had passed on the way up, this one was filthy and uncared for and all the children looked miserable and underfed. Surely, I thought, it's not the village that Gerry lived in and spoke so highly of, but it was, for Durrell started pointing out to me the various landmarks, and showed me the site where he camped. Eight years had elapsed since Gerry's previous visit to the Cameroons, and things had changed a great deal, at least politically. Now it was not unusual to find that the more intelligent members of the community were also the leading political lights, and this was the case with the old hunters who had helped Gerry on his first visit. They all sat down on the ground around us and listened carefully while Gerry talked to them and made arrangements to come back and stay for a few days. He was particularly anxious to get a bird called Picathartes, a member of the crow family, but was worried that this was not the right time of year for young birds, which are the easiest to rear. But Elias reassured him.

'Yes, Sah, sometim dis bird e get pickan for inside de house. I go look um.'

It was settled that Gerry would return the following week, leaving Sophie and me behind in Mamfe to look after the collection.

It was during our stay in Mamfe that we found two creatures who became my particular favourites: a baby bushbaby who turned out to be rather rare and whom I christened Bugeyes, or Bugs, and an equally rare kind of squirrel who, because of her minute size, I called Small. Since both of these were babies, it was my lot to look after them. Durrell was constantly sickened by the way that Sophie and I crooned over these babies. But we ignored him.

Bugs and Small ruled our lives—or rather Small ruled mine. She was a dear little thing, still blind and helpless, so she needed all the warmth and attention which I could give her. The most important thing was to construct a suitable nest which was also big enough to take a hot-water-bottle.

Eventually I found a small, square biscuit tin in which I placed a hot-water-bottle, covered with a cotton blanket, and then lined the whole thing with cotton wool. Into this I put Small. It was rather like a carry-cot and I took it everywhere I went, for, like all babies, Small had to be fed regularly and often, and also she fretted if I left her alone. To begin with her food consisted of Complan, glucose and Abidec, which were all mixed together with warm water and administered to her by an eye dropper. She was never a problem child and soon learnt to cling to the dropper with her front paws while I controlled the flow and the rest between dropper-fuls in case she got wind. She soon grew into a very lovely squirrel with an orange head and neat black-rimmed ears, and her gingery body had a rich, moss green tinge, with a line of white spots running down each side; but it was her tail that was her true glory—long and thick, green on top and vivid orange underneath, which she kept curved over her back, the tip hanging over her nose. She was absolutely tame from the moment she opened her eyes, and I could do literally anything with her; she loved to be tickled, which would send her into a trance. I had always thought she would turn out to be intelligent, a suggestion which was scorned by Durrell, and one morning shortly after her eyes had opened and we had been particularly busy, as a result of which I had forgotten her mid-morning feed, I was sharply reminded of her presence. Her carry-cot box had been left by my bed but she had somehow found her way out of this, discovered the door and appeared in the doorway of the huge living-room. Chucking madly, she came running over to me and climbed right up on to my shoulder, still complaining vigorously that she needed to be fed. She was very indignant and would not wait for me to give her the dropper but got on to the table, where I was preparing her food, and tried to climb into the cup. Eventually she was pacified but from this time on she woke me every morning by leaping on to my bed and chucking into my ear until I fed her, after which she would investigate both our beds with great enthusiasm.

'You'll have to put Small into a proper cage, you know, Jacquie, or you're going to lose her.'

I know Gerry was concerned with her safety, but I also know that he objected strongly to her rooting around in his bed and nibbling his feet.[2] Reluctantly Small was installed in a cage, one that had been especially designed for her, with a sleeping box at the top and lots of interesting bits of rotting wood that she could investigate. Once in her own cage, she developed an absolute mania for

[2] I don't mind an animal sharing my bed, but I strongly object to being woken up at 5 o'clock in the morning by an enthusiastic squirrel who is endeavouring to push a peanut into my ear. G.D.

bed-making which has never been equalled by any of the squirrels I have had since. Paper tissues were put into the sleeping box as being the safest and most hygienic material available, but she was far from satisfied with my arrangement and spent hours dragging everything out, tearing it up into small pieces, patting it, stuffing large amounts into her mouth and rushing back into the sleeping box, where tremendous noise and scuffling went on. Later, I opened the outside door and peeped inside the sleeping box, to be met by a pair of bright eyes peering back at me from a cocoon of torn tissues, but she soon forgot about me and went on with the intricate business of constructing a nest, leaving herself just enough room to get into it. Once inside, a piece could be drawn over the hole, shutting her off completely from the noises outside and any cold draughts. It never ceased to amuse me and I spent many hours watching this activity during the time we had her.

Bugs was an entirely different, rather independent character. She was fully weaned when she arrived, so did not need bottle feeding, and readily accepted everything we offered her. Insects were her favourite food and one evening she was nearly submerged by the swarm of flying ants that appeared and poured into the cages and into the house. The animal boys placed bowls of water everywhere to collect the ants as they fell, and for days afterwards we had a wonderful supply of insects to feed the animals with. During the rush to collect the ants, I heard a tremendous kerfuffle coming from Bugs's cage. On looking in, I saw her with her eyes popping, surrounded by flying ants, her mouth and both hands absolutely crammed; but this did not prevent her chasing them round and round the cage, trying to collect even more, although where she was going to put them obviously had not occurred to her. She, too, loved to be played with, leaping about the cage while I tried to catch her, then pouncing on my hand and nibbling it gently before bouncing off again. Sometimes she would become quite docile and lift up one forearm so that you could tickle her underneath, but the thing she liked best was lying on her back while you tickled her tummy and she tried, very ineffectually, to stop you.

We had stayed in Mamfe a lot longer than we had originally intended, because animals were coming in steadily, but we were forced to move out of John Henderson's house as he was going home on leave and his replacement would naturally want to take possession. John offered us a small African house just below his, with mud walls and floor and a banana leaf roof. It was a little dilapidated but after a coat of whitewash and a fresh roof, it was really quite pleasant, and there was enough room on the small veranda to take all the animals. It was very much hotter than John's, however, and infested with enormous spiders; one even crawled into Durrell's camp bed and marched across his chest one night, to his horror and my relief that it was he and not me who had been chosen. As the house had no lavatory of any kind, the usual hole was dug a suitable distance away, and night visits could be the most hair-raising affairs, for you never knew what you were going to meet, either on the way or when actually ensconced in it. The most frequent visitors were enormous cockroaches, but there were the odd spider and snake. I began to feel that if I did not leave Mamfe soon, I would go stark, raving mad, so I begged Durrell to move on to Bafut.

'Well, I must write and warn the Fon first,' said Gerry, 'but I'll do that today and send it up on tomorrow's lorry.'

So the formal note was written and was duly despatched next day, together with two bottles of whisky. We waited hopefully for a reply:

> *Fon's Palace,*
> *Bafut, Bemenda*
>
> *My Good Friend,*
>
> Yours dated 23rd received with great pleasure. I was more than pleased when I read the letter sent to me by you, in the Cameroons again.
>
> I will be looking for you at any time you come here. How long you think to remain with me here, no objec-

tion. My Rest House is ever ready for you at any time you arrive here.

Please pass my sincere greetings to your wife and tell her that I shall have a good chat with her when she comes here.

Yours truly

Fon of Bafut

Sophie very sweetly offered to stay behind for a few days and bring half the collection with her and also the bulk of our equipment, and we promised her faithfully that we would arrange for her to come up to Bafut as soon as we possibly could.

The road up to Bafut was dreadful, full of ruts, deep potholes and rocks, but it was fascinating country. At the beginning we passed through the thick forest in the river valley—large trees like skyscrapers covered with lianas— and this time we did see the odd bird : hornbills, touracous and the vividly coloured pygmy kingfisher. Hundreds of tiny streams seemed to bisect the route and these were crossed by rickety wooden bridges; crowds of African children played in these little streams, shrieking and waving as our convoy passed, and clouds of beautifully coloured butterflies swarmed on the damp banks. Gradually the road began to climb, at first without seeming to do so, until suddenly the forest gave way to the vast areas of grass-lands which swept, bleached white by the sun, towards the horizon. As we looked back, the forest lay behind us and at last I could appreciate it, free of its claustrophobic tentacles; but still the red dust swirled around us and poured into the lorry through every crack and crevice, so that by the time we eventually arrived, late that evening, outside the Fon's compound, we looked exactly like Red Indians.

It felt deliciously cool after the heat of the forest road and the cloying humidity of Mamfe, and in the dim evening light I could just make out the vast courtyard and the cluster of huts which made up the Fon's compound, and to the right of us, at the top of what looked like a vast series of Inca-type steps, the Fon's imposing Rest House. This was not unlike an Italian villa, shoe-box shaped with a wide veranda and a neatly tiled roof. But we had no time to waste gazing around us.

'Come on now, let's get all these animals unloaded and settled on the veranda and fed before it gets really dark.'

The boys bustled around unloading our equipment, leaving us to get the animals established on the coolest side of the veranda, and Pious, who was getting the kitchen staff organised, brought me some warm water to mix the babies' milk with. Tilley lamps were lit, a snack meal prepared, and, after a real lick and a promise, we all fell exhausted into our camp beds.

The next morning a messenger appeared bearing a letter from the Fon :

My Good Friend,
   I am glad that you have arrive once more to Bafut. I welcome you. When you are calm from your journeys come and see me.

> Your good friend,
>> *Fon of Bafut*

Most of the morning was spent rearranging the animal cages, cleaning and feeding them and getting ourselves organised so that we could deal adequately with any animals that might be brought in within the next few days : we also had to arrange for Sophie to join us as soon as we possibly could. However, it was essential that we paid our respects to our host.

We made our way across the courtyard to a smaller one, dominated by a large guava tree, beside which was the Fon's own villa—a small replica of the Rest House that we were staying in. At the top of the few steps stood the Fon of Bafut himself. He was a tall, slender man, dressed in a plain white robe with a blue embroidered edge, and on his head was a small skull cap in matching colours. He was obviously absolutely delighted to see Gerry.

'Welcom, welcom, my friend, you done come.'

'Yes, I done come back to Bafut. My friend, you are well?' Gerry inquired.

'Foine, foine,' and he did look well.

Then I was introduced to the Fon and we must have looked a weird pair for his 6 feet 3 inches towered above my 5 feet 1 inch, and my small hand disappeared completely into his great, well-shaped one.

'We go for inside,' he said, gesturing that we follow him into the villa.

It was a pleasant room, cool and simply furnished with a few leopard skins on the floor and beautifully carved wooden sofas piled high with cushions. As we sat down, one of the Fon's wives came rushing forward with a tray on which was the inevitable bottle of whisky and some glasses. At we clutched our tumblers, filled practically to the brim with neat White Horse, Gerry delicately broached a difficult subject.

'My friend, I do fear come back to Bafut because some man done tell me that you get plenty angry for me because I done write dat book about dis happy time we done have together before.'[4]

The Fon was obviously surprised and displeased and demanded to know, 'Which kind of man tell you dis ting?'

'Some European done tell me in Bua.'

'Ah, European,' replied the Fon, shrugging his shoulders, faintly surprised that we should believe anything a white man told us. 'Na lies, dis. I never get angry for you,' he continued, topping up our glasses. 'Dis book you done write, I like um foine. You done make my name go for all the world. Every kind of peoples e know my name, na foine ting you do. Dat time I go for Nigeria to meet dat

---

[4] I had been told that local politicians had informed the Fon that I portrayed him most unsympathetically as a drunkard and womaniser.

Queen woman, all dis European dere e get dis your book and plenty plenty people dey ask me for write dis ma name inside dis book.'

We were both delighted and astonished for we had been assured that the Fon had taken the whole thing as a tremendous insult, but we did not pursue it, and asked him how he had liked meeting the Queen.

'I like um too much, na foine woman dat.' Then he laughed. 'Na small, small woman same same for you,' pointing at me, 'but e get power time no dere. Wah, dat woman get power plenty.'

We went on to ask him how he had liked Nigeria.

'I no like,' he said firmly, 'e hot too much, I shweat, I shweat, but dis Queen woman she walka walka, she never shweat, na foine woman dis.'

He was enjoying reminiscing on his trip to Lagos and went on to tell us how he had presented the Queen with a carved elephant's tusk as a gift from the people of the Cameroons.

'I don give dis teeth for all dis people of Cameroon,' he explained, 'dis Queen she sit for some chair an' I go softly softly for give her dis teeth. She take um. Den all dis European dere dey say it no be good ting for show your arse for dis Queen woman, so all de people walka walka backwards. I walka walka backwards. Wah! Na step dere, eh? I de fear I de fall, but I walka walka softly and never fall—but I de fear too much.'

I managed to catch Gerry's eye, as I was getting anxious; not only did I want my own lunch, but I could see we would be there all day if someone did not make a move. The Fon made us promise that we would come back that evening. Smiling broadly at me he said, 'For evening time I go show you what kind of happy time we get for Bafut.'

Trying to smile back equally broadly, I said, 'Good, good.'

When we returned to the Rest House, we found a large group of people waiting on the back steps, one of whom was clutching a calabash which he thrust at us, saying, 'Massa, massa, look um.'

Very carefully, Gerry removed the banana leaves that were stuffed in the mouth of the gourd.

'Now whatee dere for inside?'

'Na squill-lill sah.'

'A squill-lill,' I said wonderingly, 'what's that?'

'I don't know.'

'Well, don't you think you had better find out just in case it's something lethal?'

'Yes, I suppose so.'

'Na bad beef dis? E go chop me?'

'No sah at all. E be pickan.' And there, curled up at the bottom lay a tiny squirrel, a few inches long.

'Well, do you want to keep it?' said Gerry, looking at me over his shoulder. 'It will probably die, you know.'

'Of course I want to keep it. After all, you thought Small was going to die and she didn't.' And so yet another forest squirrel joined the nursery of baby animals that I had clustered in the corner of one of the rooms in front of the Tilley infra-red heater. Although she did not become anywhere near as tame as Small, Mamfe, as we called her, would allow herself to be scratched as a very special favour.

After dinner, and armed with two Tilley lamps and two bottles of whisky, we presented ourselves in front of the Fon's dancing house. How different the evening air was after Mamfe. Here, although it was warm it was bearable, and there were even evenings when you could use a light blanket on your bed. I soon found that even my sweat rash had begun to disappear, which was an asset for it did not improve one's public image to be seen scratching the most unfortunate parts of one's anatomy. The Fon looked marvellous, dressed in a scarlet and yellow robe and, of course, clutching the inevitable tumbler full of whisky.

'Tonight we all go for have a happy time,' he announced, and soon we were all seated in a row at one end of the dancing hall. This looked rather like a Territorial Army drill hall with white-washed walls. At one end there was a row of imposing cane chairs on a small raised dais under the watchful photographs of all the members of the Royal Family from Queen Victoria onwards. The Fon gestured that we should be seated, with Gerry on his right hand. In front of us was a table with the usual bottle of whisky and tumblers. The royal band arrived consisting of four youths and two of the Fon's wives, carrying such varied instruments as drums, flutes, a gourd filled with dried corn and other odd items. These were closely followed by a line of women—some of the Fon's wives. The Fon turned to Gerry, smiling,

'My friend, you remember dat European dance you done show me last de time you done come for Bafut? How you go call um—de conga? Well, I go show you something.'

He raised his hand and the band began to play something that had a familiar rhythm and the line of Fon's wives began to move. Suddenly it dawned on me that this was the Bafutian version of the conga. Durrell seemed very touched by this display, and when the dance finished he said,

'Dis is a fine thing you do for me.'

At this the Fon roared happily. I complimented him on his band and on his dancing wives.

'Wah no, dis my wives tire me too much. Dey humbug me too much.'

'Gerry says I humbug him too much,' I replied.

'Your husband catch lucky, he only get one wife, I get plenty and dey humbug me time no dere.'

'Well,' I replied practically, 'no wives, no babies.'

This amused him tremendously. He laughed so much that I began to get worried that he might have a stroke or something, but he did recover and, with tears streaming down his face, he patted Gerry thunderously on the back and said,

'Dis woman your wife get brain.' Then, digging me in the ribs and patting me on the head, he said, 'You be good wife for me.'

Fortunately this conversation was cut short by the band launching themselves frenziedly into yet another hectic rhythm.

'Why don't you get up and dance with him, Jacquie?' said Gerry. I was horrified. Admittedly I had learnt the mysteries of the cha-cha on the boat coming back from the Argentine but this man could really dance and had what all Africans seem to have naturally—a truly wonderful sense of rhythm which no European could ever match.

'Don't be silly,' I said, 'I can't possibly. He's about three times my size, anyway. We'd look ridiculous.' But Durrell was not thwarted. He leant across me to the Fon.

'My friend, you go show dis dance for my wife?'

'Yes, yes, na foine,' and before I realised what was happening I was on the floor. The band was playing a tune very similar to a samba, so I quickly offered to teach this to the Fon. He was in very high spirits and we were soon whirling round the floor at a great rate. No doubt it would have mystified Latin American dance experts, but whatever it was, it was great fun. Gerry told me later that we had looked 'very funny', for I was almost completely hidden by the Fon's flying robes so that at times it looked as if the Fon had grown another pair of feet and was dancing round by himself. After half an hour of this I was about ready to drop when, as a special treat, the Fon rewarded me for my efforts with a large calabash of special *mimbo*—the local palm wine. I had already had the misfortune to sample this much-treasured brew, which looked like weak milk, smelt like burning rubber and tasted like nothing that I could possibly describe; to sum it up it was just plain revolting. Five calabashes were presented to me, all of which the Fon carefully tasted, and when he eventually decided which was the better vintage, he gave me a tumblerful. What could I do? There was no convenient aspidistra for me to empty it into so, taking a deep breath, I managed to swallow a whole mouthful and, what is more surprising, smile brightly at my host and assure him that it was, without doubt, a very fine *mimbo*. As he continued to watch me closely, I had no alternative but to go on sipping it appreciatively.

'Will you allow your wives to drink with me?' I asked.

'Yes, yes,' and he waved them forward. With grateful thanks I poured the rest of the *mimbo* into their outstretched hands.

Before any of us realised what time it was, dawn had broken, and I honestly felt that my head had, too. The Fon insisted on escorting us right to the bottom of the steps of the Rest House.

'Goodnight, my friends,' he said, 'you done give us happy time.'

Sophie joined us later in the week and arrived looking very exhausted, but relieved to be in the cool climate of the grasslands. As we now had quite a lot of animals we decided to divide them up into three lots—mammals, birds and reptiles—each of us with our own particular section to deal with, and we quickly developed a very simple routine. Tea would be brought to us at first light—usually about 5 a.m.—and the baby animals would then be fed and their bedding changed; then would come general inspection. Each animal would be examined very carefully before any cleaning out was done, and the things we had to notice were how much food had been eaten or left, if the droppings were good, and whether there were any peculiarities in general behaviour which might mean that it needed medical attention. All cleaning we tried to finish before breakfast was served, and this left the rest of the morning free for us to wash the pots, prepare the feeds, and arrange with Philip, our cook, to go to the local market and buy us any other supplies we needed. If there was any time left, the film camera was set up and this kept us busy until lunchtime. A sleep after lunch was an absolute necessity, especially in view of our hectic night life with the Fon. After tea the evening feeds were done, and sandwiched in between all this we fed the baby animals, dealt with new arrivals and, what was more important, attended to any sick or injured creatures that had been brought in. Perhaps the most pathetic patient we had during our entire stay in Bafut was a large female chimp who had been caught by hunters in a wire snare. Both her wrists had been cut down to the bone and gangrene had set in. We carefully cleaned the cuts and packed them with sulphur powder, and we also gave her a shot of penicillin, but the most marked thing about the animal was its lethargy and also the skin colour. The Bemenda area was fortunate in boasting both a government medical officer and a veterinary officer and we sent a message to them both to come and look at this chimp. After a thorough examination they decided to take some blood samples, because the vet was convinced that the animal had sleeping sickness.

'Most interesting,' he said, 'but I'm afraid you are wasting your time trying to save it. Thanks a lot, anyway, for letting us know. I'll arrange with the U.A.C. people when the report on the blood comes through to let you know. Incidentally, if I can be of any help to you any time, don't hesitate to let me know, although you seemed to be doing pretty well for yourselves from what I saw.'

The chimp died the following day and the blood test confirmed the vet's diagnosis, so we could comfort ourselves with knowing that we could have done nothing whatsoever to save it. Happily, the rest of our medical work consisted mostly of dosing creatures for internal parasites, removing jiggers—these were a very common parasite, which afflicted monkeys' hands and feet and could easily be removed with the aid of a safety pin. There were a few broken limbs, mainly due to rough handling or badly set traps, and there were often animals suffering from severe dietary deficiencies. The latter condition taught me yet another thing about wild animals : contrary to the popular belief, they do not live in a Utopian state where all their whims and fancies are catered for; in fact some of them were in appalling condition when they came to us.

Perhaps the high spot of our visit to Bafut was the night when the Fon made Gerry a deputy Fon and presented him with a complete set of his own magnificent robes; this was a

tremendous honour, especially as our host made no secret
of the fact that he despised almost all Europeans.

I had to excuse myself halfway through the enormous
party that was given to celebrate this unique occasion for,
shortly before, a disturbing influence had entered our
happy community in the shape of a small, wizened baby
chimpanzee. To begin with, he was an endearing little soul,
looking rather like a Japanese doll. Sophie, as was to be
expected, doted on him, and it was a constant battle to
discipline him at all in face of her pleas that he was only
a baby. As he grew in size, he also grew in mischief. The
only one who had any real control over him was Gerry,
but even his patience got a bit thin when, at the crack of
dawn, Cholmondeley began to play games by rolling all
over the bed, leaping about and generally being a great
nuisance. A remarkable thing about this chimpanzee was
his memory and his ability to learn things very quickly.
He shared, I am happy to say, Durrell's bed and not mine,
so it was essential that he was trained not to wet the
bed. After one or two false starts, he did learn to hang
his nether regions over the side of the bed whenever he
wanted to spend a penny, although in his enthusiasm he
sometimes failed to make it. Another chimpanzee, Minnie,
was wished on us by a local coffee planter, and Durrell
spent a wonderful day trying to coax her into the crate that
we had taken with us in the back of the Fon's Land-Rover.
She was quite rightly very suspicious and reluctant to have
anything to do with either the crate or us, and so Gerry
devised a type of parlour game to entice her in. I could
only admire his tremendous patience; it took the entire
day to get Minnie into that crate, and although she dined
extremely well on a wide variety of succulent fruits, we
had nothing all day but a bottle of beer and a couple of
bananas. When we released her in the special Dexion
cage back at the Rest House, she took it very calmly. She
was a very sweet creature, though when she wanted our
attention she would scream as only a chimpanzee can.
This was fine, as nobody in the Fon's compound was

greatly disturbed by noise, but I began to wonder what would happen on board ship and when we got her back to England. Still, as Durrell constantly said, we would face this problem when it arose.

It was with very mixed feelings that Sophie and I prepared to leave Bafut. It was agreed that she and I would travel down the British side of the Cameroons with the bulk of the delicate stuff, leaving Gerry to come down on the good tarmac roads of the French side with the reptiles and the main bulk of our equipment. U.A.C. again came to our aid and sent up two Bedford trucks, one of which was a four-wheel drive. We were particularly grateful for this, as the rainy season had just begun and the roads could be practically impassable at times. Sophie travelled in the bigger truck with the really delicate things, while I followed in the smaller one with the hardier stuff and our personal baggage. Our first stop was to be Mamfe. This part of the trip was relatively straightforward and a little rain had dampened down the dust so that by the time we reached Mamfe and presented ourselves at the U.A.C. bungalow, we were relatively clean. John Henderson had already left, but his Assistant, John Topham, and his wife laid everything on for us and without them we could have done very little. The Tophams were very concerned about the next step down to Kumba, and John warned us, 'It's essential that you get up early tomorrow and leave as soon as you possibly can, for our drivers think that it's going to rain heavily later on in the day and they want to get the main part of the journey over before the road starts disintegrating. I've fixed up your accommodation at the Rest House and after you've had dinner here with us, I'll drive you over. Now don't worry about the animals, for I'll get my watchman to keep an eye on them.'

We were deeply grateful to the Tophams for they also helped us feed the animals so that we could finish it all quickly and get to bed.

The next day we got up very early, fed all the animals, cleaning out the creatures who need it most, and were ready to leave within an hour. With luck we should be in Kumba, at the head of the good road, by early afternoon, and then we could really clean out the animals properly and give them a full forty-eight hours' rest before continuing down the road to Tiko, where we were to join the ship. But we then found that two of our stewards, one of whom was Sophie's great favourite, had not turned up as arranged. Our poor drivers were beside themselves with fury, and reluctantly agreed to send the other boys out to look for them. It was obviously going to rain soon, and just as I had decided that we would have to leave without them, the two stewards shame-facedly appeared. The drivers were all for dealing with the culprits there and then, but my only thought was to get away.

'Let's leave any arguments until we get to Kumba,' I said, 'but I promise you that I'll deal with them severely and they won't be allowed to forget it.'

As I feared, the rain came down in torrents and the road was like a glue-pot, the soft African red dust turning very quickly into a glutinous mud which made all driving extremely difficult and dangerous. The farther we got down the road, the worse the road conditions became, and eventually it began to look for all the world like a tank training ground, with deep ruts and small streams of water everywhere. But I was not prepared to see the big Bedford truck sliding all over the road and then slewing right off it at right angles, ending up with one side in the ditch. We stopped as quickly as we could and as I lowered myself on to the ground I sank into mud up to my ankles, but I was far too concerned about Sophie and the animals in the truck to be worried about my boots and trousers. With the help of all the boys and the drivers we eventually got Sophie out. She was very shaken but had suffered nothing worse, and, like me, was concerned about the animals in the back. Gingerly I climbed up to have a look and, as far as I could tell from the angle, they seemed to be all right, though we could not do anything until we righted the vehicle. By this time I was in a furious temper and was hardly in the mood for dealing pleasantly with two Mammy wagons which had appeared, screaming Africans demanding that we move out of the way and let them pass. I sent one of the boys to tell them to shut up and come to help us. He returned quickly.

'Madam,' he said, 'dat man he say he not fit to come help us.'

'Why not?' I demanded.

'I no savvy.'

'Well, I bloody well will,' I shouted, and stormed towards the two wagons. Then followed an almost Gilbertian scene during which I swore, cajoled, argued and finally indulged in a long political harangue, the gist of which was how could they possibly hope to get independence and govern themselves when they could not even help a fellow traveller on the road. Strangely enough, this appeared to tickle their fancy for they all suddenly shouted 'Hooray', got down, removed the planks that formed their seats and, within fifteen minutes, our lorry was on the road again and we were all congratulating each other on how wonderful we all were. When I tried to apologise for my bad language they insisted that all I had said was true and that they were pleased that I had no fear, and had told them.

A quick look in the back of the truck confirmed that everything was all right there, so I suggested that we get to Kumba as soon as possible and get the poor, frightened animals settled down for the night. It was a most cheerful convoy that made its way down to Kumba and we were all sorry to say goodbye to our Good Samaritans when we eventually reached the house of a Doctor Crewe at the Filaria Research Laboratories who had kindly offered to accommodate us for the night. The entire collection was unloaded and we set about our task of cleaning all the cages and examining the occupants more carefully, but all they were interested in was being fed and allowed to sleep. Sophie and I lay in our beds that night and agreed heartily that neither of us would want to repeat that journey. We marvelled that the animals had stood up to it so well.

'You see,' said Sophie, 'Gerrykins will have had a perfect journey. It will be sun all the way.'

'Anyway,' I laughed, 'it's jolly good practice for the boat journey home.'

The trip from Kumba to Tiko was very uneventful, and what a blessing to travel all the way down on a paved road. At the Rest House in Tiko all our charges were housed underneath us. We had a four day wait here until the banana boat sailed, and I was thankful, for it did give both the animals and us a breather we certainly needed after that hair-raising trip. Needless to say, Durrell turned up eventually, having had a perfect journey down—no rain, no incidents and it was not even too hot.

'Seems that we are always the mugs, doesn't it, Jacquie?' observed Sophie. 'Well, we'll let him do it next time, if there is one, that is.'

Earlier in the trip, when we had been considering what we would do with our animal collection when we eventually reached England, I, in a fit of demented enthusiasm, had suggested to Durrell that we keep this collection and use it to blackmail the Bournemouth Council into giving us a suitable zoo site in the town. This had given Gerry a new lease of life, and all I could hope was that Bournemouth Council were in a blackmailing frame of mind.

Our voyage home went reasonably well, except for a brief force eight gale off the coast near Dakar, when I was the only conscious member of our group and struggled manfully for two hours tying tarpaulins which had worked loose in the gusts. Dear Cholmondeley was allowed, unbeknown to the Captain, to spend his time in Durrell's cabin—Sophie and I were sharing one and Durrell was sharing with somebody else. All the stewards adored this chimp and allowed him to get away with absolute murder; even when he did a large pooh in the middle of the bunk, they cheerfully cleaned up all the mess and changed the bunk. The rest of the crew were also very helpful, except for one crank who, for some reason or other, disapproved of both us and the animals. This man threw a large bucketful of feeding pots overboard, and on the night before we disembarked at Liverpool opened the doors of all the cages he could, throwing the cages off the hatch on to the deck. The only results of that outburst was the death of a newly born baby black-eared squirrel and the drowning of another squirrel which dashed overboard in its fright. I think Durrell would have murdered the culprit if we had managed to catch him.

'People who work off their grudges against helpless things like animals and children make me sick,' he fumed. This was the first time that anything like this had happened to us for normally sailors adore animals and cannot do enough for them.

It was the final stage of our journey that nearly finished us all off—at least the human beings. A goods van had been arranged to transport us and our collection the entire way from Liverpool to Bournemouth and we had naturally anticipated that we would go from Liverpool to London hitched on to a regular passenger service, and then be coupled up with a train from London to Bournemouth. But no, this was far too simple, and in the end it took us fourteen hours in the goods van, being shunted off and on to trains, in and out of sidings, with only one seat between three of us, before we eventually reached Bournemouth. The only one who really enjoyed it all was Cholmondeley, who thought it was wonderful to have three human beings to plague all night. The fact that we were all three hungry, tired and thirsty, made no impression upon this delightful animal. He had had his food and milk and was quite happy to be nursed by whoever was sitting in the one seat.

Furniture vans met us at Bournemouth Station and quickly conveyed us to the house in St. Albans Avenue. Cholmondeley we handed over to Gerry's mother, who was delighted to have him, while we erected our large marquee on the back lawn to accommodate the majority of the hardier animals. The delicate ones we put in the garage which Sophie's brother had lined and insulated for us. The animals seemed no worse for their ordeal, and only wanted to be fed and left alone, while all we wanted was a hot bath and a drink and a good meal. But it was many hours before either Gerry or I got it. Cholmondeley was finally put to bed in a large laundry hamper after being thoroughly spoilt by Gerry's mother and sister, and it was only then that we were free to crawl up to our flat and collapse.

'You always wanted a zoo in our luggage, Durrell, well, you've certainly got one now,' I said.

CHAPTER 5

Our backyard zoo was at first welcomed by our neighbours, who enquired assiduously as to the welfare and general health of our 'friends', and we did do our level best to keep the whole place neat and clean and, what is more important, fly-free. All the hardier creatures, like civets, mongooses and the bigger monkeys, were housed in the large marquee on the back lawn and for the birds of prey we constructed a special shelter out of Dexion, which was then covered by the tarpaulins that had been donated to us by Smiths of Poplar, and made to our own specifications. The really delicate creatures like squirrels, some birds and bush babies, lived in the garage which Sophie's brother had prepared. The reptiles were a tremendous problem but here Paignton Zoo came to our rescue, offering to house everything. This was a great relief for we could never have provided the type of heated quarters they needed. To begin with, Minnie, our large chimp, lived in the huge cage that we built, but her habit of screaming continuously all day resulted in showers of protests and so here again Paignton Zoo was our saviour.

Actually the whole thing was extremely well organised and certainly none of the animals suffered in any way whatsoever except, perhaps, from an excess of attention.

Jacquie and Gerry Durrell preparing for their first trip together: Argentina, 1954

The garden at Bournemouth

New Zealand 1962: Jim Saunders, the Durrells,

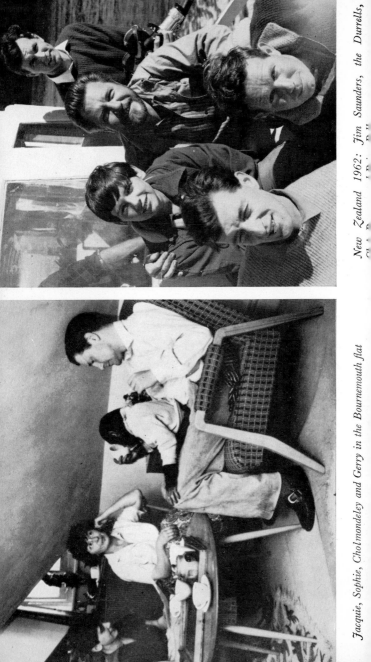

Jacquie, Sophie, Cholmondeley and Gerry in the Bournemouth flat

Bafut. Jacquie feeding a Putty-nose Monkey

Morning inspection in Bafut

Whirling with the Fon

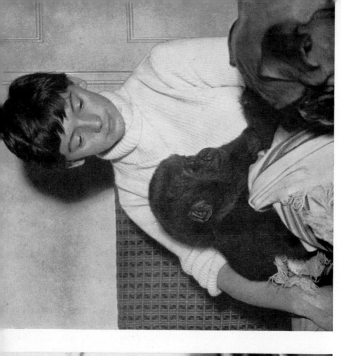

With the young gorilla N'Pongo

With Dingle the Chough

With N'Pongo in the garden of Les Augrès Manor

Les Augrès Manor

With Larry Durrell and Cholmondeley in Jersey

A local greengrocer proved himself to be a most valuable supporter and kept us supplied with the weird variety of fruit and vegetables that we needed—often, I feel, to the detriment of his own pocket—and a nearby pet shop never failed to produce all the meat we needed. Perhaps the most helpful authorities were the R.S.P.C.A. and the Sanitary and Health Inspectors, all of whom had to visit us within the first few days of our arrival in order to satisfy their departments that our accommodation and disposal arrangements were adequate. They passed us on every count, in spite of a neighbour who insisted that our animals had infested her chickens with fleas.[1]

Cholmondeley naturally lived in the height of luxury in the house, surrounded by fawning females who allowed him to get away with everything. The only discipline he ever received was from either Gerry or myself, and unfortunately his head was soon turned by the constant procession of people from press, television and passers-by, who all wanted to meet this fiendish creature. His day was a quite simple one; he was awakened in the morning with a large cup of milky tea and then dressed in the exotic sweaters that my mother-in-law had knitted for him 'to keep the cold out, dear'. Then the rest of the day was spent in plaguing the inhabitants of the house until he was finally put to bed in the evening with the aid of a large mug of Ovaltine, leaving everyone else exhausted and irritated beyond recovery. At first he slept in Mrs. Durrell's room, until we found out that she did not read at night in case the light disturbed the furry monster. We quickly removed him to our own room, where he soon learnt to accept light, noise, cigarette smoke and anything else without detriment to his health or well-being. His favourite game was to swing on the curtains in the front living-room, where he held audience every day for all the children in the neighbourhood. He also befriended the small son of one of the tenants in Margaret's house, and they had a wonderful time together,

[1] Which bears out my contention that all neighbours are obscene and should not be heard. G.D.

D

playing with wheelbarrows, although it usually ended up with poor John Hawker, red-faced and puffing, wheeling the great lump of chimp round the garden in his wheelbarrow. Another favourite haunt of Cholmondeley was the golf links at the end of the avenue. Here, he would climb trees, turn somersaults, chase Johnnie the dog and divert the attention of some harassed golfer, often to the detriment of his handicap. Worn out with his play, he would then be placed in the Hawkers' push-chair and, looking like an Eastern potentate, be wheeled ceremoniously back to the house—again usually by young John.

In between entertaining Cholmondeley St. John, we entertained members of the local and national press, who listened sympathetically while Durrell outlined his scheme for a zoo in Bournemouth. The City Fathers were amenable to the whole idea and one or two departments even suggested suitable sites, but these, unfortunately, proved on investigation to be useless, for one reason or another.

It was at this period that we made our first really serious attempt to break into television, when we were given an introduction to Tony Soper who was at that time producing 'Look'. As a result of this, Tony came to Bournemouth to see all the film that we had shot in Bafut and, after a great deal of hard work on his part, cutting and shaping the film, our first series, 'To Bafut for Beef', was launched. It was deliberately off-beat in its presentation and it was a serious attempt on Tony's part to get away from the normal two people sitting in hard chairs, gazing inanely into a camera and indulging in a not very enterprising cross-talk act. Our flat was reconstructed in the studio and it was so successful that Johnnie, our dog, accepted it completely as home, but we made the unfortunate mistake of gearing the three programmes to Cholmondeley who, like all animals, never behaves as you want him to. It was my opinion that our dear chimp was by now so full of himself and his own importance, having appeared on television many times in such august programmes as 'Tonight', that he had become pompous and was determined to let no one else have a chance. Anyway the series was received by critics and viewers alike with very mixed feelings, but at least from our point of view it was worth doing as it taught us a great deal about both television and ourselves. Perhaps the most important thing to emerge from it all was the fact that Durrell was not happy in a television studio, and if he was going to pursue any career in this particular medium, he would have to be filmed on location and not asked to perform in a studio. I personally adore television but we both look upon it purely as a shop window to display the importance of conservation.

When we were all beginning to despair of ever finding the ideal site for our zoo, we received a letter from the Town Clerk of Poole; apparently his Corporation were intrigued with the idea of a zoo and had an excellent site. Durrell pursued this with vigour and enthusiasm, for the year was drawing to a close and the weather would, in a very short time, become too cold to keep any animals out of doors, so it was essential that something be done quickly. Anyone who has ever dealt with local Fathers will know how frustrating this can be, and the adverbs 'quickly' and 'speedily' do not apply to their activities. The site they had in mind was quite lovely—an old Georgian house and grounds on the edge of Poole Harbour itself. It was perfect in every way, except that the house had unfortunately been neglected very badly and would need an awful lot of money spent on it to make it habitable. This also applied to the outbuildings and the gardener's cottage, which really needed knocking down and rebuilding completely. Still, we persevered, and during the next eighteen months spent an awful lot of time and money trying to find a method of satisfying the Council's various demands, and pressuring our bank in London to lend us £10,000.

It soon became obvious that we were never going to complete arrangements in time to settle the animals that winter, but Durrell hit upon a very good idea.

'Why don't we persuade one of the local big stores to have

a small zoo in their basement as part of their Christmas activities?'

'It's worth a try,' I agreed, and eventually J. J. Allens offered us some very reasonable terms. They would construct, to our design, a series of cages in their lower basement with a specially designed centre-piece as a nursery for dear Cholmondeley. We, on our part, would supply the necessary animals, an attendant to clean and feed them and, of course, all the food; any takings would be divided equally between us. We were far too desperate to argue but thought that if we could at least pay the wages of someone to look after the animals, it would be one way of solving our problem. The rest of the animals could go to Paignton Zoo, and we were deeply grateful to the zoo authorities for feeding and housing our animals which for so long had bitten deeply into our meagre capital, and also, preoccupied with the Poole negotiations, Durrell was not in a mood to begin writing a book.

The Allens venture went extremely well—that is until one Sunday morning when we were all relaxing and thanking heaven that we did not have to go down that day, when the telephone rang. Margaret rushed into the room:

'Gerry, that's the Bournemouth Police. Something's wrong at Allens. Can you talk to them?'

Durrell shot out of his chair. Eventually he came back into the room struggling into his coat.

'That bloody baboon Georgina has somehow got out of her cage and is creating havoc in the windows of the store. I phoned for a cab and you all follow me down,' and with this he rushed off. When we all finally arrived at the store we had to fight our way through spectators who had gathered to peer through the window. Georgina was having a lovely time, bouncing on the beds and leading everyone a merry dance inside. A very harassed Durrell came rushing towards us.

'You and Margo guard this entrance while I and the two constables try to corner the animal.'

All the people, inside and out, served to encourage Georgina in her activities, and she was revelling in all the attention, but she finally realised that Durrell was, on the contrary, getting extremely annoyed and angry. Georgina had always been a natural coward, probably due to the teasing and beating she had received when appearing as an amusing 'turn' at the African bar from which we had rescued her. Suddenly she wrapped herself round one policeman's leg and began to scream. Under Gerry's instructions the constable stood quite still, while Gerry disentangled Georgina from his leg and rushed her back into her cage.

'Cor, I thought I'd had it that time, sir,' the poor bobby said, mopping his brow.

'You behaved extremely well, and I want to thank you all for all your help.'

'No trouble at all, sir,' he assured us, 'and it makes a change from teenagers, I must say.'

The poor store manager, hurriedly summoned from his home, pottered about assessing the damage that had been done, which was fortunately negligible when one considers what could have happened, but we spent the rest of the day sitting nervously by the telephone, waiting for another call from the store—happily we heard nothing.

The remaining part of our stay at Allens passed uneventfully and the zoo proved such a success that it was kept on for a few weeks after Christmas. The income we received proved to have covered our feeding costs, but none of us was really sorry when it closed down. Our greengrocer friend came to our assistance in a different way this time and put his van at our disposal to ferry all the animals except Bugs and Small down to Paignton Zoo, and soon our neighbours were beginning to smile at us once more.[2] After all the fevered activity of the past few months it seemed strange to be able to lie in bed until 8 a.m. in the morning and not have to rouse oneself at first light to go and see that the animals were safe, nor have to worry about the weather or grapple, as we did one moonlight

[2] See footnote page 97. G.D.

night, with the guy ropes of the marquee, which the
unexpected gale force wind was threatening to destroy.
Cholmondeley also stayed with us in Bournemouth, being
far too spoilt to send to a zoo, but Gerry's mother loved
him and treated him just like a child, giving him everything
he wanted; even Sophie, who should have known better,
was just as soft with him, and I found her one day pacing
up and down the living-room with the ape perched on her
head.

'Well, he likes it,' she replied when I remonstrated with
her, 'and after all he's only a baby.'

Our negotiations with Poole Council dragged on endlessly
but eventually we did reach the basis for a suitable agreement, and Hart-Davis agreed to guarantee the £10,000
bank loan on the understanding that the zoo would provide
material for an endless series of books, for which they
would have exclusive rights.

However, the lease when it came proved to be quite
impossible. It was quite clear that the majority of the
£10,000 would be swallowed up by specified repairs to the
house and outbuildings alone, which was not our intention
—after all, we had to construct the various enclosures
and houses that would be necessary and install heating,
lighting and other essential services. Durrell was bitterly
disappointed and we reluctantly came to the conclusion
that we would have to abandon the whole idea of starting
a zoo in Poole. Poole Council felt that we had let them
down very badly, but they could not appreciate how much
time and money the negotiations had cost us, and also how
necessary it was that we undertake another trip that year
if we were going to keep pace with the demands of our
publisher. Poor Durrell was beside himself with worry.

'If we don't do something very soon, all those animals
now at Paignton will be lost.'

We had an agreement with the zoo that if we did not
reclaim our animals by a certain date, they would revert
to the zoo. This was a very fair arrangement for, after all,

they had housed and fed these animals for the greater part of that year.

'Why don't we go on another trip,' I suggested, 'and get away from all this muddle and mess?'

Gerry leapt at the idea, and it was decided that we return to the Argentine, but this time concentrate on that country alone.

There were several problems to solve before we could go, the main ones being the future of our zoo and what we would do with Cholmondeley who was, by this time, becoming rather difficult for anyone to handle except Durrell.

'Let's go ahead with the Argentine trip idea anyway. We can deal with the question of the zoo and Cholmondeley when we've made final arrangements to leave.'

So Sophie and I pushed ahead. The B.B.C. were very keen on the trip, though they did not feel that they could send a cameraman with us. However, they did offer us a contract for any film that we might take ourselves. All our old friends at the Foreign Office and the Argentine Embassy were approached again, and were all as helpful as they had been four years before.

'I think we ought to give Hart-Davis another book, you know, before we go anywhere, but I honestly don't feel that I can write up the African trip yet awhile,' said Durrell.

'What about publishing all those talks you did for the B.B.C.?'

'Which talks?'

'You know, the ones you did called "Encounters With Animals". You know how popular they were and how many people wrote asking for copies of them.'

'Do you think Hart-Davis would like that?'

'Well, at least it's better than nothing,' I persisted, 'and anyway, Spencer will tell you.'

Spencer thought it might be a good idea, but asked to read the scripts first before committing himself finally. When he did give his approval, it was a fairly easy task to assemble the stories together and link them with a small,

introductory piece. Ralph Thompson produced some enchanting drawings to illustrate the book, and much to
everybody's surprise except mine, the book was well
received and was a modest success.

'Nothing like getting money twice,' laughed Sophie, 'but
I don't think they'll allow you to get away with it again.'

Nevertheless, it did give Hart-Davis something to produce
during our absence.

But our main concern was arranging the details of our
trip. Gerry was obsessed with Darwin's book, *The Voyage of
'The Beagle'*, and had a secret ambition to go to Patagonia
to see for himself the penguins, fur seals and elephant seals
that live along its coast.

'I've never lived among a group of large animals before,'
he said, 'and it should be fascinating.'

Sophie and I merely exchanged glances.

'At least it would be a great change from zoos, banks,
rates, surveyors and councils,' I laughed, 'and I think I'd
rather be discussing collapsible cages again and the state
of the roads.'

Rovers were approached about supplying us with a
Land-Rover for advertising purposes, but they felt, quite
rightly, that there was hardly any value as the South
American markets are always restricted; but they did
offer to supply us with a special expedition model with
double tanks and other refinements at a reduced rate,
which was a great help, and we also got a trailer on the
same basis. This time I would see to the booking of the
passages myself, as I did not want a repetition of our first
voyage. Poor Durrell had had a miserable year one way and
another, and I thought the voyage out would do him a lot
of good. Blue Star were extremely helpful and offered us
accommodation on one of their cargo boats.

I thought that the matter of the zoo had been shelved
entirely, but I had overlooked Durrell's stubborn nature.

'Surely there must be somewhere left that has sensible
people in charge who are not hidebound or tied up with red
tape and the dear old town and country planners,' Durrell

moaned bitterly one day. Before I realised what I was saying, I found myself suggesting the Channel Islands.

'They've got a better climate than ours and their own government, so I think they're worth trying.'

'That's a jolly good idea, but we don't know anybody there who can help us, and time's getting very short.'

We did get help, from a most unexpected quarter. Durrell called in to see Rupert Hart-Davies to thank him for all his help with the bank loan and to explain why he would not be needing it. He was as heartbroken as we were at our failure over the Poole site.

'Surely you can find another site, Gerry? There must be plenty of them.'

'You're probably quite right, but you still have to get over the planning problem wherever you go in Britain. Jacquie suggested Jersey, but the snag is that we don't know anyone there.'

'But I do,' said Rupert. 'An old army chum of mine lives there and I'm sure he'll do everything he can to help you. I'll write to him today. You never know, he might pull something out of the hat for you.'

Rupert's friend was only too willing to help, and soon we were on our way to Jersey where Major Fraser was waiting to take us on a conducted tour of the entire island to look at various properties that he knew were on the market. For one reason or another, however, none of them was really suitable. We could not afford to pay the tremendous prices then being asked in Jersey, and so we had to find somewhere that could be rented on a long lease, and that had outbuildings which could reasonably be converted into animal houses.

'Don't despair, old boy,' said the Major, 'let's go back to my place and have a drink and talk about it.'

Les Augrès Manor was a lovely property, built entirely of granite, its imposing block shaped like a square U with a beautiful granite 15th-century archway at the end of each bar. Hugh Fraser was obviously very proud of the property and lovingly showed us around the granite outbuildings.

There was a cider press, cow sheds and garages and a lovely walled garden, one of whose granite walls was covered with rockery plants. There was also a large pond and a sunken water-meadow.

'What a delightful place this is, Hugh,' said Gerry.

'Yes, I think it's one of the loveliest properties on the island,' our host replied. Durrell turned to me and laughed.

'Wouldn't this make a nice zoo?'

'Yes, it certainly would,' I said.

'Are you serious?' enquired Hugh.

'Well, I was serious about it making an excellent zoo site, but surely you wouldn't entertain the idea.'

'I would, dear boy, as I'm finding the upkeep of this place a little too much for me, and also my wife feels that she wants to move back to England.'

'But I couldn't possibly afford to buy it, Hugh.'

'No, no, of course not, I mean to rent it to you. Let's go inside and talk about it, anyway, over a drink.'

So, almost at the last moment, we redeemed our animals and Paignton Zoo very kindly agreed to go on housing them until such time as our zoo was ready. Hugh Fraser promised to get things moving with the Island authorities, as we had barely a month left before we were due to sail for the Argentine.

We made another trip to Jersey a few days later to meet the then head of tourism, Senator Krichefski, who received both us and our idea most enthusiastically and promised to give it all his support. Other officials we saw were equally helpful and appreciated the need for speed in concluding the formalities. Hugh Fraser's advocate drew up a suitable lease which was signed literally twenty-four hours before we sailed from Plymouth. In the meantime Gerry had approached a former associate of his, who had agreed to manage the place and be responsible for establishing the zoo.

'I would have loved to have stayed in Jersey and built the place myself,' said Gerry wistfully, as we watched Plymouth slip away.

'I realise that, but your own life has to go on, you know, and particularly now that you have mortgaged your future to establish this place. Anyway, you'll have the satisfaction of bringing your animals back to your own zoo, and surely that's worth knowing.'

CHAPTER 6

It was wonderful to be back in Buenos Aires again and to see the jacaranda and bougainvillæa in full bloom, although on the night of our arrival it was pouring with rain. It was impossible to clear all our equipment from the Customs that night and so it was decided that we would take such as we could and come back the following day to clear the rest. Bebita had arranged for us to stay at our old hotel and she was waiting for us when we got there. Everyone seemed delighted to see us again, even the hôtelier and his staff.

On this trip Sophie was with us once more, and we had taken Mrs. Durrell with us to do the round trip, as she had not been well and the doctor thought a sea voyage would prepare her for the winter ahead. She and Sophie fell in love with the city, as we knew they would. Bebita shocked us by saying that she was on the verge of leaving the Argentine for good and going to live in New York when our letter had reached her, announcing our arrival, so she had put off her departure for a week in order to see that we were well settled before she left. This gesture was typical of Bebita and we were heart-broken at the thought that she would be leaving us soon.

After recovering from the effects of arriving and seeing all our friends once more, Gerry and Rafael rushed off to the docks to see about getting off the rest of our equipment and the Land-Rover, and then began our flirtation with the Argentine Customs. Our first visit had taken place during the rule of Peron when his official blessing on an enterprise had removed all snags from the path, and made entrance into the country extremely easy and trouble-free. However, in the intervening years, Peron had been removed and replaced by a more democratic government, as a result of which no one was prepared to take responsibility for allowing us and/or our equipment free entry into the country. The fuss they made about such valuable items as old clothes and second-hand tarpaulins had to be experienced to be believed. They quite calmly released our cameras, half our cine film and our Land-Rover, but held on, for some unknown reason, to the trailer, all the animal collecting equipment and the remainder of the film. It took us a whole month of argument, cajoling and daily visits to the Customs House to secure the final release of everything. The situation was quite ludicrous, for the Embassy in London had given us their official blessing, as on the previous trip, and had also endowed us with all the trappings of an official scientific mission, but no one in the Argentine itself was prepared to accept this. Fortunately, I did not take part in the sallies on the Customs House. Durrell had to attend and lead the attacks, and I am assured by all the poor unfortunates who went with him that his Anglo-Saxon was well to the fore and that the entire Customs House seemed to be peopled by the Garcia family.

While we were waiting for the tenth Mr. Garcia to make up his mind whether or not we could have the rest of our stuff, we spent our time pottering around Buenos Aires itself.

'What we urgently need is a driver for our Land-Rover,' said Durrell one morning, 'for I'm not risking my neck driving around here. You Argentinians are all maniacs on the roads.'

And so it was that Josefina entered our lives. She was small, with a thick mop of curly auburn hair; her brown eyes were enormous and her brilliant smile gained her many a parking place. She was a first-class driver and a marvellous companion. Our only regret was that she would not be able to come with us on our trip down south—that is, if we ever got there. To drive around Buenos Aires with Josefina at the wheel was the most hair-raising experience, relieved only by her voluble attacks on the poor hapless driver who happened to disagree with her. With shaking fists and an absolute stream of Spanish invective, she would leave the poor individual in absolutely no doubt as to what she thought about him and his ancestry. She also, unfortunately, picked up some of the fruitier Anglo-Saxon phrases that Durrell was wont to strew around when pressed; it was a little shattering to hear Josefina call somebody a 'blurry bastard' in her imperfect English.

To relieve our bewildered souls from the monotony of trips to the Customs House, the de Sotos suggested that we spend a day at their *estancia* just outside Buenos Aires. We took Mrs. Durrell with us as she still had a few days left before she had to return to her ship. The vehicle was bulging with de Sotos and it was brother Carlos who took over as driver. Our trip to 'Segunda' was a marvellous break and it did do our souls good, watching the birds on the lake behind the house and riding over the pampas. Mrs. Durrell was particularly thrilled at seeing at least one of the places that we had told her about and she did not turn a hair when our vehicle began sliding about in the mud caused by a recent downpour. It is an extraordinary thing about the Argentine roads that they quickly become like glue-pots, even after the slightest fall of rain, and under the hot sun revert as quickly to being quite solid and hard, although, like Africa, dust is everywhere.

We were all very sorry to wave goodbye to Gerry's mother, but it had been a nice break for her and had given her the opportunity to meet all our friends.

Our battle with the Customs continued unabated, though there did appear to be a slight gleam of hope in as much as the head Mr. Garcia had promised to see Gerry the following week. As we had another week-end ahead of us, the de Sotos suggested that we go back to 'Segunda'. This time it was a lovely day and it was very pleasant just pottering about, taking the odd still photograph and bird watching. Whilst the rest of the party were drinking *matte*, the herb tea so common in South America, I decided to clean out the Land-Rover, which was full of fag ends, toffee papers and thick dust. The Land-Rover at that time had the normal hard-top doors at the back, the top half sliding upwards and the tailboard either being supported by chains or dropping down completely. For some unknown reason I must have been extra energetic, for my vigorous gestures loosened the catch on the top half of the door, and as I was standing back to admire my handiwork the heavy door fell down on my head. Cursing madly and feeling a little dazed, I decided to finish my housewifery; at this point Durrell appeared to find out what I was doing.

'Nothing,' I said, 'just cleaning out the back.'

'You look very pale. Are you all right?'

'As all right as I can be when the top half falls on my head. Otherwise I feel fine.'

He just grinned and rubbed the bump that was beginning to materialise.

'Leave things alone and come and sit down. A bit of dust won't hurt us anyway.'[1]

We returned to Buenos Aires to find that on the Monday morning a Señor Dante had suddenly decided that we could have all our equipment immediately. Any efforts to discover what had persuaded them to relent so suddenly were useless. Either no one knew or else they preferred not to tell us.

'Just be grateful that you have got it all out of their hands at last,' said Rafael's sister, Mercedes, 'and don't bother to ask them all why. Just take it and go.'

- The next person we consulted about our trip south was Dr. Godoy, head of the Fauna Department in the Argentine

[1] My wife has never learned the basic philosophy of life, that if you leave things alone one of two things happens. Either they cease to be of any importance whatsoever, or else they assume such magnitude that you have got to deal with them. If the latter happens you are prepared, by virtue of the fact that you have been relaxing while they gained magnitude. G.D.

Ministry of Agriculture, and he advised us to go down to Puerto Deseado where we could contact a certain Captain Giri who knew where the penguin colony was and would be willing to help us get the film that we needed.

'But where are the elephant seal and fur seal colonies?' asked Gerry.

'Those you will find on the Peninsula Valdéz, but in order to get on to the peninsula you must go to Puerto Madryn, where the seal hunters, whose names I will give you, will show you exactly where to find the colonies.' He then showed us some aerial photographs that had been taken of the seal colonies earlier that year and this enthused Durrell tremendously.

'I can't wait to get out there,' he said. 'I've always had a "thing" about seals and actually to live amongst them must be wonderful.'

No one else shared his enthusiasm.

The other problem that faced us was to find a driver who knew the road down south reasonably well; we also needed an interpreter—Rafael could not accompany us this time for he was studying at the university to be a veterinary surgeon and could not get away. However, he suggested that his cousin, Marie Renée, might be willing to do this, providing we could wait until the end of the year when she had her annual holiday from the civil service. A meeting was arranged between us all to discuss this.

In the meantime I began to feel rather peculiar and one night in a restaurant I nearly fainted, a thing I had never done in my life before. As all members of the de Soto family seemed to be doctors, it was not difficult to persuade one of them to have a look at me.

'It is quite obvious what has happened,' he said, 'She has mild concussion as a result of a blow on the head, so I suggest she spends a couple of days in a darkened room, and keeps very quiet, with no excitement. If she is no better at the end of the week, please let me know and I will arrange for some X-rays to be taken,' and smiling sweetly he departed. He was quite right, for in two days I felt really well again and was soon buzzing around, trying to get things organised for our departure.

Marie Renée had agreed to come with us and had also found us a driver, a young lawyer called Dicky Solo, who knew the area reasonably well but who could only drive us down there—he could not stay. This did not worry us very much, for we felt that between us we could manage to drive ourselves back to Buenos Aires. Eventually a departure date was set—early morning, 1st January. This amused all the rest of our friends, as they felt that nobody would be in a fit state to leave Buenos Aires on New Year's Day, but they had not reckoned with our enthusiasm. Just as everything was arranged, however, we had an accident. Josefina was at the wheel, driving us all round to Marie Renée's place for a drink before taking us on to a cocktail party, and as usual she was chattering madly and not really concentrating on the road. As we approached the only set of traffic lights in Buenos Aires, they changed, and it was apparent to me, sitting in front, that Josefina had not noticed this.

'Lights!' I shouted, and the next thing I knew was that I was being thrown forward into the windscreen, then grabbed by Durrell, who pulled me towards him. Streams of blood flowed over the pair of us. I was only interested in finding out whether the Land-Rover had been damaged or not. We had apparently hit the stationary car in front of us, hence my being hurled into the windscreen. People appeared from everywhere, all shouting and offering help, and the vehicle was soon surrounded. I still felt perfectly fine, except for the blood which was slowly covering us both.

'Josefina, drive quickly to my house,' said Marie Renée, 'so that my father can look at Jacquie's head.'

'Shouldn't we take her to a hospital?' said Sophie, who had been quite badly shaken herself.

'No, it's all right, dear. If my father can't treat her

himself he will recommend which hospital we should take her to, but be quick, Josefina, we must stop this blood.'

Marie Renée's father was, unfortunately, a heart specialist, and had no facilities whatsoever for dealing with an accident like mine, so he sent us round to a nursing home he knew of, after telephoning to warn them. By this time I was feeling pretty awful and it was obvious to everyone that I was very badly shocked. At the nursing home, they quickly took me into the operating theatre and examined my head. It was apparently quite a tiny cut but, like all head wounds, had bled profusely. Anyone looking at Gerry and me would have thought we had been in a massacre. They eventually put five stitches in my forehead and told me to take things easily and come back in a week's time when they would remove the stitches. Strangely enough, I felt no pain whatsoever.

'Don't worry, tomorrow you'll feel awful,' prophesied Durrell comfortingly, 'and I wouldn't be surprised if you have a couple of black eyes.'

Poor Josefina was very upset by the accident and blamed herself.

'Don't be a silly girl,' said Durrell, 'it wasn't serious. Let's all go and have a drink to celebrate.'

All the time that I had been in the operating theatre they had allowed Gerry to stand beside me. He had stood there, rather white-faced, holding my hand and I was quite sure that he was far more upset about everything than I was.[2] Before braving our cocktail party we decided to stop at a café and have an enormous brandy each.

'I don't honestly think that we look presentable enough to go to a cocktail party, do you, Durrell?'

We both looked at our blood-stained clothing ruefully.

'There's no time for us to go back to the hotel now and change, so what we had better do is go round to their flat, explain what happened, and then leave straight away.'

[2] As a matter of fact, I was trying at this juncture to remember whether we had paid up her life assurance premiums. G.D.

They were a bit shaken by our grim appearance but quickly appreciated the situation and insisted that we come in and have a strong drink. Everyone was terribly sweet and reluctant to let us go, but by this time I was beginning to feel that all I wanted was to lie down peacefully in the dark, away from everyone. The following day I spent in bed, eating very little and doing nothing, but I insisted on getting up the day after that and remained on my feet—without black eyes—from then on.

We three got up bright and early in the morning of the 1st, but there was no sign of either Marie Renée or Dicky. 'So much for our early start,' I said. 'I bet those two never left the party and are now sleeping off their drunken orgy.'

We sat and waited for them and eventually, at about 6.30, two very tired-looking individuals appeared at our bedroom door.

'Are you sure that you want to travel today?' enquired Durrell. 'If you'd rather wait until tomorrow, I don't mind.'

This seemed to jerk them back to life, for they both protested vigorously that although they might look half asleep, they were fit to travel, so we loaded up the Land-Rover and the trailer leaving just enough room for Sophie and me in the back, and Gerry, Marie and Dicky piled in the front. It was a really lovely day and the morning sky was suffused with a pink glow that portended a boiling hot day, so I was not sorry to be seeing the back of Buenos Aires.

Dicky was a charmer and kept us all amused by talking absolute nonsense all the time, but he was an excellent driver, and after the blood-curdling efforts of Josefina it was quite a pleasure to be driving towards Mar del Plata. This is *the* resort in the Argentine. No one who is anyone would be seen dead in Buenos Aires in the months of January and February; they migrate in two directions—southwards to this rather nauseating resort or westwards towards the mountains and Bariloche. Our arrival on the

sea front caused quite a commotion, for our Land-Rover
had been bedecked with the legend DURRELL EXPEDITIONS,
a gold dodo and a list of all the trips that Durrell had
ever taken part in, emblazoned on the sides. Everyone
seemed to want to meet us; we were assailed from all sides
in various languages and, for some unknown reason, they
could not comprehend what two Argentinians were doing
with an English expedition. Still, it gave a good opportunity
to have several beefsteak sandwiches and some beer, and
to top up our Thermos flasks with hot black coffee. Dicky
had a half hour's sleep and it was pleasant to sit there,
watching everybody apparently enjoying themselves. We
planned to make landfall that night at a small town called
Nicochea, where some friends of ours lived. Needless to
say, we had not warned them that we were coming, but we
assumed that they would be pleased to see us and could
get us into a hotel. This was nearly our undoing for we
had not reckoned with the holiday traffic again, and it was
only after tremendous persuasion on the part of one of
our friends that we all got a bed that night.

We resumed our trip at around 10 o'clock next day,
feeling that we could all do with a long lie in, and made our
way down to a city that I have quite a fondness for, Bahia
Blanca. This is situated at the foot of the bulge on the
right-hand side of South America and is a very important
focal point for it is from here that the roads branch either
westwards towards the Andes and Chile, or southwards
towards Tierra del Fuego and Patagonia—it also, regret-
tably, marks the ending of any sort of paved road. We
arrived there sooner than we had expected and decided to
push on as far as we could. Soon the pampas gave way to
the harsh scrubland of Patagonia and we left the paved
roads for ever, from then on travelling along roads that
were alternately dirt or stone enlivened by corrugations.
Durrell swore that he would have a permanent twitch at
the end of our journey, if all the roads in Patagonia were
like this. There were a few fairly level bits without the
corrugations, but alas, not many, and in spite of Dicky's

careful driving we could not avoid bumps, potholes and
jolts, and soon I had a permanent headache and my back
and neck felt as though a rather vicious horse had kicked
them. No amount of padding with blankets could protect us
from the jolting, and soon we all became almost inured to
it.

We were making for Patagones, the place mentioned
by Darwin in *The Voyage of 'The Beagle'*. The only thing
was, being very dark and very wet, we could not find our
way into the wretched town which was slightly off the
road, and in his enthusiasm Dicky nearly drove us into a
lake. However, we did eventually decide which way to
go and soon found ourselves in the dimly lit plaza. Now
to find a hotel. The only inhabitant who apparently wanted
to know us was the policeman and he was extremely polite
and helpful and advised us strongly to stay at the Hotel
Argentina, which we would find round the next block.
Thanking him profusely, we drove round the next block
and eventually found a rather unimposing edifice which
appeared to be closed and shuttered. For half an hour we
hammered at the doors and shuttered windows, and by
this time hysterics had broken out among us. With tears
streaming down our faces, we got out of the vehicle and
walked round and round the building trying to find an
entry—which Dicky eventually did. We all went inside
while Dicky went back to bring the car into the enormous
courtyard that he had found. Lights suddenly appeared
everywhere, and, trying desperately to control her laughter,
Marie Renée explained to a rather blowsy female who had ·
appeared clutching an oil lamp, that we needed five beds.

'But of course, Señora,' she said, 'we have had very few
guests, please go and choose your own rooms.' So we spent a
hilarious half hour going into each room, trying all the beds,
while Marie Renée kept chanting like a Greek chorus
that they were sure to be filled with either fleas or bugs
and she certainly was not going to lie on any of them.
Eventually we chose our room, at the front of the hotel,
and Sophie decided to have the one next door; Marie

Renée said she would have a room to herself, although she probably would not sleep, she assured us, and Dicky could not have cared less.

In the meantime, the owner of the hotel appeared, grasping platefuls of wholesome ham sandwiches and bottles of beer, for which we were most grateful as we had not had a decent meal since that morning. We found that the bathroom was opposite us, and since the water was beautifully hot, Durrell and I determined to wash some of the Patagonian dust away. This again appalled Marie Renée, who was convinced that we would end up with some foul disease, and I am sure the fact that we did not bothered her a great deal.

The morning light showed Patagones to be rather a charming place and we had, in fact, chosen the best room in the house. It was small but very clean and the beds, though rather of the hospital type, were extremely comfortable. The long windows opened on to a tiny balcony which, in turn, overlooked the street below, and we could see the Rio Negro glittering beyond.

'Well, I think it's charming,' said Durrell, 'and I'm delighted that we decided to stay here.'

We woke the others up and we all went down to the dining-room below, where we consumed lots of hot coffee, toast and that gorgeous Argentine sweet, *dulce de leche*, which tastes, to my mind, just like liquid fudge. Feeling very much better and very full, we took a fond farewell of the Hotel Argentina, clambered back into the Land-Rover and rattled our way across the rather imposing river which separated the rest of the Argentine from Patagonia proper. As we went along we could see the occasional Patagonian hare racing us along the road—a delightful creature who sits up kangaroo-fashion on his hind legs to watch you go by—the odd armadillo, and the ridiculous pheasants that have no road sense whatsoever and yet, remarkably, never seem to get knocked over by any passing vehicle. I found this landscape intriguing; it was barren, harsh, arid and continually windswept, but there was something about it which gripped you. It was almost as if the land was whispering to you.

The weather, again, was very mixed, alternately fine and pouring with rain. When we reached the tiny port of San Antonio Oeste, we decided to stop and eat a proper lunch, and found a nice little café which was prepared to serve us a meagre meal of soup, enormous beef steaks and chips, followed of course, if we wanted it, by *dulce de leche*. We wasted two hours here, but we thought it worth while to stretch our cramped limbs before launching ourselves on the last-but-one stage of our journey to Puerto Madryn. Our contact here was the manager of the Hotel Plaza, but unfortunately we arrived late in the evening and were pushed into very Spartan accommodation. But we did not care, for the beds again were comfortable and we were all completely worn out, especially poor old Dicky who had driven non-stop for hours over very tiring terrain.

The next morning we met the manager who quickly rounded up the two seal hunters and they took us out to a nearby cliff where, through binoculars, we could see a quite biggish colony of these magnificent creatures. But they assured us that the only real place to see both the fur and elephant seals was, as Godoy had said, at the far tip of the Peninsula Valdéz. It was impossible for us to stay at that time, for it was essential that we reached the penguin colony as soon as we could, otherwise they might all have left. But we promised to be back within ten days.

Our trip to Deseado took us through the big oil port of Comodoro Rivadavia, which was booming at this particular time, owing to the recent oil concessions granted mainly to Americans, allowing them to exploit the oil deposits in the area. Because of this boom, beds were impossible to find and eventually Sophie, Marie Renée and I shared a double bed, while Gerry and Dicky slept in the Land-Rover. We were not sorry to leave Comodoro. The country after this was quite strange and for a long time we passed through black sand dunes. We decided to press on without stopping, and reach Deseado as early as we possibly could. We found the hotels that the manager in Puerto Madryn had recommended but here too they were bulging with oil men, and we were forced, all five of us, to sleep in the Land-Rover that night. The next morning revealed the delights of Deseado; it was cloudy, dull, cold and windy and it looked for all the world like a Hollywood western ghost town.

'Whoever christened this place "Desire" must have been really desperate,' Dicky observed.

We could not find accommodation anywhere until, quite by accident, we met the local Post Master who, we discovered, was of British descent and spoke English very well indeed. As he was a pillar of local society, such as it was, he took it upon himself to badger all the hotel keepers into offering us accommodation, but they could not help us, so he then went to the Agricultural Club and pestered them to give us a couple of rooms. While we were wrestling with the bed problem, Dicky had ferreted out the local airline representative and had ascertained that a plane was actually leaving in about an hour's time. We were all deeply sorry to see Dicky go, but I think he was secretly glad to be going back to the fleshpots of Buenos Aires.

Captain Giri was also found by our Post Master friend, and he promised to arrange for us to stay on an *estancia* right near the penguin colony. Señor Huiche, on whose *estancia* we were going to stay, presented himself at the Club the following afternoon. We discovered later that he was half Indian and this probably accounted for the great kindness and civility that he showed to us during the few days we spent with him. He told us that he was more than delighted to have us all go and stay on his *estancia*, and it was agreed that we would leave the very next day. To lighten our load, we arranged with the Club manageress to leave our trailer in their yard and also that she would keep our rooms free for when we came back.

The Huiche *estancia* was perfect; he himself had built it several years earlier, and although it was simple and lacked a lot of the civilised 'essentials', for Sophie and me at any rate, it was like being in another world. The house itself

was in a dip, but he had an enormous expanse of beach
which bordered his property, and Sophie and I spent hours
walking up and down with only the odd sheep and the
occasional oyster-catcher to keep us company. The sea
was a magnificent emerald green and bitterly cold. It was
perfect peace after the bustle of Buenos Aires and the
squalor of Deseado, and neither Sophie nor I felt that we
ever wanted to leave.

The penguin colony could be smelt long before we ever
saw it and nothing is quite like the sweet, fishy smell of these
birds—certainly no bird is quite so stupid. The colony
stretched for miles in all directions and there was no
problem about filming them; they did not care about us
and were obsessed by the important functions of breeding,
going to sea to get food, and feeding their young. The area
looked exactly like photographs of the moon and was
covered with their small nesting craters which they dug
themselves. The main body was situated behind a very high
sand dune, over which these silly birds had to walk in order
to get to the sea and the fish. It was a tremendous effort
for such small birds to scramble up one side, constantly
exposed to the fierce sunlight, though they could toboggan
down the other slope. It must have been at least a four-
mile walk, all told, and certainly not one that I would
cheerfully do regularly. The one thing that I found difficult
to understand was why they should spend the hottest time
of the day standing in the sun panting, instead of sitting
inside their cool burrows. The other thing that worried
me was the high mortality rate, for desiccated bodies of
baby penguins were everywhere, and did not appear to
have died as a result of predators. The climate was also
rather moonlike in as much as that, in the shade it was
bitterly cold and in the sun you could be burnt rather
badly. I cannot say that I was sorry to leave the penguin
colony, for to my mind the birds lacked personality and
were certainly nothing like what penguins in the zoo had
led me to believe their wild relatives should be. Even now

I can never see these unfortunate birds without a feeling of deep sorrow.

When we were not filming the penguins, we were all down on our hands and knees, searching the sand dune for evidence of the Patagonian Indian settlement that Huiche told us had existed there, and we found many beautifully made and highly coloured arrowheads, skinning utensils, and even a set of the old hunting *boleadoras* (three balls on a string which when thrown at an ostrich or a guanaco wraps itself round their legs and brings them down). In the sand valley behind the dune, Gerry came upon an Indian skull.

'What a pity these wonderful people no longer exist. Why is it that so-called primitive people and the wild life have to go to the wall in the face of progress?' Durrell remarked bitterly.

Marie Renée translated the gist of this to our host, who replied by saying that the place always made him feel sad for he felt that the lonely spirits of the Indians were still lingering.

'They are all around us, but I feel much sorrow for these spirits, as they are so unhappy.'

He was quite right, the whole place was pervaded by this feeling of sorrow and unhappiness.[8] Still, the penguins did not seem to be affected by it as they waddled to and fro across the dunes, undisturbed by the stupidities of the human animal.

We thankfully turned northward again and made our way to the Peninsula Valdéz and the colonies of fur and elephant seals. The Peninsula itself was fascinating and quite different in both coloration and landscape from the rest of Patagonia, which was flat and almost monotonously devoid of life. Instead, here was undulating land with large green bushes covered in small yellow blooms, and even the road was a different colour—red instead of grey. The area

[8] It was not so much a feeling of unhappiness as a feeling of gentle melancholy. G.D.

also seemed to be populated with a wide variety of wild
creatures : six gingerbread-coloured guanacos, relatives of
the llama, watched us unperturbed as we drove past, but
soon hurried away when Gerry tried to film them, obviously
thinking that we, like so many local farmers, wanted to
shoot at them; armadillos scampered alongside madly; little
ground plovers ran in and out of the bushes as we passed,
and many small and highly coloured birds flew around us as
we bumped our way across the corrugations towards the
estancia at Punta Norte where we hoped to get information
and, far more important, water—a difficult commodity to
come by in Patagonia.

Reaching it at last, we were greeted with great enthusiasm by the three peons who lived there. Strangers were
always a welcome distraction from sheep and we were soon
offered food and wine and they refused even to listen to
our many questions until we had finished the excellent
roast lamb that they had given us. Marie Renée briefly
outlined what we wanted to know and why we had come
to the Argentine. They were fascinated and, I think, a little
appalled to think that we had bothered to come all the
way from Britain to catch and film their animals, but they
readily offered to help us in any way they could. Finding
the fur seals would be easy enough, they said, for they
still had their pups and lived packed together on the beach
not far away from the *estancia*, but the elephant seals were
a more difficult problem. They had already had their pups
and had left their normal maternity area, so might be
anywhere along the coast-line or even not there at all,
but they did have their favourite haunts and these they
marked on our maps.

We were not despondent and fell to finding a suitable
camp site, which we discovered not far from the fur seal
colony; our friends promised that they would willingly
supply both water and meat whenever we needed it. Our
camping site was in a small depression just below the road
and we soon got ourselves organised, dug a fire pit and,
after making a cup of tea, decided to turn in. We three

females huddled in the Land-Rover while Durrell slept underneath it, protected by a tarpaulin. Sleeping in a short-wheelbased Land-Rover is no easy matter and it took some time for us to sort ourselves out, but we did finally, and all fell into a sound sleep.[4]

Durrell had lit the fire and made coffee by the time we disentangled ourselves from the vehicle next morning and while we sipped this very welcome brew he told us about his early morning visitor, a large male guanaco, who apparently had not taken too kindly to finding a disgusting human in his territory and had belched and snorted vigorously before departing as swiftly and silently as he had come.

'Magnificent beast,' announced Durrell, 'and what a shame that they are so persecuted.'

As we sat there drinking our coffee and meditating on our plans for the day, a weird noise came floating from the beach.

'What on earth is that?' Marie Renée asked.

'Fur seals, I hope. Now hurry up and finish that coffee and let's go and have a look. We didn't come all this way for you to sit around staring into the fire. While you lot were sleeping, I made sandwiches and filled the two flasks, so we needn't bother about lunch.'

Durrell was being very forceful for so early in the morning, and before we realised it we had unhitched our trailer, filled the Land-Rover with cameras, film and food, and were bumping in the direction of the noise.

'Don't drive too near the edge of the cliff, Gerry, or we'll all end up among the seals. Let's leave the vehicle just here and walk to the edge.'

Strangely enough, he agreed with me and we all cautiously approached the cliff edge, clutching binoculars and cameras.

'Just look at them all,' shouted Durrell against the ever-

[4] I would strongly advise anyone who has not slept under a Land-Rover in which three women are all snoring in different keys to circumnavigate the experience should it offer itself. G.D.

present wind. 'Aren't they bloody marvellous?' And indeed they were a breath-taking sight, but there was so much going on below us that we did not know where to look first.

'There's a dear little baby,' exclaimed Sophie, pointing at something that resembled a liquorice jelly-baby.

'Isn't that a magnificent bull?' Durrell urged, indicating a massive creature who was lying there, snout pointing skywards, and surrounded by a clump of adoring golden female seals. But it was the noise that was overpowering. It hit us as we reached the edge, sounding exactly like a volcano about to erupt, with the sea noise acting as counterpoint, and the colours were staggering. These lovely, rich brown and golden creatures, shimmering in the sun and lapped by an emerald green sea with vivid green weed-covered rocks as a background. I just sat, watching and listening. Soon Durrell was busy shooting foot after foot of film, changing lenses rapidly and cursing if even a tiny cloud crossed over the sun. He was drunk with pleasure and so madly in love with the seals that it was with the greatest difficulty that we prised him away from them after several days in order to go and look for the elephant seals.

A hectic two days' driving up and down the coast, visiting the various sites that we had been told about, brought nothing. Gerry was beside himself.

'It looks as if we were too late and they've gone down to Tierra del Fuego,' he moaned.

'Still, let's keep looking,' Sophie replied. 'You never know.'

Our patience was rewarded. We were trudging along the shingle beach in a school crocodile, carrying all our equipment, when we came to an area covered by huge grey rocks and boulders. Hoisting ourselves and our packs over these, we dropped down on to a small beach surrounded by peculiarly shaped boulders. We were out of breath and stopped to eat a sandwich.

'Don't give up hope, Gerry,' I pleaded, 'you might find some tomorrow.'

'No, it's my own stupid fault for not coming along here first instead of spending so much time on those fur seals. They've gone south by now, I know, I just feel it.'

During this speech I had been kicking at the shingle, and one of the pebbles hit a boulder a few feet away, which gave out a deep sigh and opened a pair of huge, limpid eyes and gazed at us.

'We're surrounded by them,' I gasped, and sure enough there were about twelve of the gigantic creatures around us —they had just lain there quite calmly while we almost picnicked on their backs. On closer inspection we found that there were three males, six females and three well-grown babies, the latter about 6 feet in length whereas the females were approximately 14 feet, but it was the males that were most impressive, being between 18 and 22 feet long, and having the true trunk-like nose which gives these seals their name. They lay there, quite unconcerned, as we photographed and measured them and even walked right up and peered into their faces.

'The problem is that I'm supposed to be taking moving pictures—so how do we get the things to move?'

'Well, they do move a bit when they flick wet shingle over their backs with their flippers,' I offered.

'Yes, but I want them really to move into the water and rear up as they're supposed to do.'

Marie Renée soon solved this problem by throwing handfuls of fine, wet shingle on to their tails, and after a little while one of the huge males decided that we were being a nuisance—rather like a fly constantly landing on your nose—so he reared up right in front of us, hissing like a reptile, and moved slowly backwards into the sea behind with a caterpillar-like movement. This was all that was needed to spur the rest on, and soon they were all rushing backwards into the welcoming green sea and were gone.

Sadly we returned to our camp to prepare for our journey back to Buenos Aires. Leaving us to finish clearing up, Sophie disappeared seawards to wash her 'poor aching feet in that lovely cool water'. A few seconds later she reappeared, absolutely sopping wet and giggling madly.

'You'll never believe it, Gerry,' she said, 'but I was chased by an elephant seal along the beach and I fell down a hole and got drenched.'

Still, she didn't seem to mind being wet and it almost seemed as though this was retribution for disturbing the peaceful slumber of the elephant seals.

Durrell drove extremely well all the way back to Buenos Aires and we dreaded the hot city again after the cool spaces of Patagonia. During the last half hour of our trip I had begun to feel very ill, with a constant headache and backache, and it was only with an effort that I managed to see the trip through to the end. Sophie had been well aware of how I was feeling, but Durrell had been too taken up with his filming really to pay much attention, and in any case I was determined that nothing should prevent him from finishing the filming. Nevertheless, it was with mixed feelings that I returned to Buenos Aires.

The humid heat was unbearable and this, on top of feeling ill, made me realise that the wisest thing for me to do was to return to Britain as soon as I possibly could, before I became a burden to Sophie and Gerry. I had already discussed it with Sophie and she had agreed that it was the best thing to do, but how to break it to Durrell was a different matter. However, he reluctantly saw that it was sensible and as luck would have it, there was a Royal Mail boat sailing in two days' time, which had a single berth still free. I felt very guilty at having to leave them, particularly as the main burden would now fall on Sophie, but she assured me continually that she could manage, and Gerry seemed confident that they would get through the rest of the trip without difficulty.

As we said goodbye on the ship, I thought how glad I was not to have missed Patagonia. I would never forget the perfect peace and silence, and the wonderful animals on Peninsula Valdéz. I was determined that we should go back there again some day.

CHAPTER 7

My voyage home was uneventful and restful, and the osteopath I saw when I got to London assured me that my decision to return home and leave poor Durrell and Sophie had been the right one. So I felt considerably better about it all.

The first thing I did on my return to Bournemouth was get in touch with the manager at the zoo to see how things were progressing, and arrange to fly to Jersey. It was a fascinating stage of the zoo's development and everyone was working feverishly to complete the site for the Grand Opening in a month's time. I was a little perturbed to notice that Gerry's blueprint for the development had not been followed, but this was not my concern and I decided to leave it until Gerry could deal with it himself.

In the meantime, I occupied myself by arranging for our flat in the house to be altered and decorated. It was fun making plans and buying new furniture. I ran a plumber to earth who could do all the alterations that were needed to provide a kitchen, and I persuaded one of the zoo decorators to stay on a little longer. By some miracle he managed to complete the decoration of the whole flat in ten days, and by the evening of the tenth day the whole place looked and smelled far better.

My biggest problem was finding a carpet large enough to fit the living-room, and curtains long enough for the windows, and I dashed backwards and forwards between Bournemouth and Jersey, trying to make the place habitable for Gerry's return in June. He had asked me to leave the move until he got back, but I thought it would be a pleasant surprise for him to find everything ready. This was the first time we had been separated since our marriage, and because I had so much to do I barely noticed it. Durrell often phoned me from Buenos Aires to make sure that I was still in existence, and, charming though this idea was, I had a mild shock when I received a bill for seventeen guineas.

I had not realised just how much rubbish we had accumulated in our small flat over the years, but I eventually found a reasonable contractor and the day came when I watched all our goods and chattels being stacked into the two railway containers. I was full of a great sadness at having to leave that friendly house after all these years; still, Gerry's mother was coming to live with us in Jersey, and Sophie would be there too, so the old atmosphere might linger a little in our new surroundings.

Despite all my careful planning, there was a last-minute rush to get everything straight before I dashed over to London to meet Gerry's ship, but I made it, and was standing on the quayside as the *St. John* sailed through the lock gates. My first shock was to see that Durrell had sprouted a ginger beard.

'I grew it for you,' he said, 'so I hope you like it.'

I did, but I had a sneaking suspicion that he had also grown it for his own convenience. The fact that it made him look rather like Ernest Hemingway and certainly every inch the public's idea of a big-game hunter had not occurred to him, and I did not have the heart to say a word. Sophie was looking very fit but tired, and I soon heard how some of the darling animals had played her up on the voyage; she had obviously given in to all their whims and fancies. On one occasion, during quite heavy seas, the ship had lurched suddenly and Sophie had ended up, backside first, in a large black rubber bucket full of dirty water.

'It's a jolly good job it was rubber, though, otherwise I might have damaged my rear end quite severely,' she observed with great seriousness.

Durrell was torn between talking to me and fussing over the loading of his animals on to the British Railways van which would take them to Waterloo Station *en route* for the Southampton steamer. I remembered the Land-Rover.

'Where is it?' I asked.

'Oh, down in the hold.'

'When are we going to get it off?'

'Well, yes, I've something to tell you about it.'

Fearing the worst, I waited.

'We had a slight accident just before we sailed and I'm afraid we damaged her a bit.'

Fortunately, I had arranged with the Rover Company that the vehicle should be taken to their London garage for them to vet, which was just as well for apparently she was not really fit to drive. By way of reassurance, Durrell went on to tell me that the other man had come off the worst and that his car was a complete write-off.

'Whose fault was it?' I enquired tenderly.

'Not ours,' protested Durrell. 'The idiot shot straight across the road in front of us and we couldn't miss him. We thought we had killed the poor man but the Argentinians must be like the Greeks—the harder they're hit, the lighter they're injured. Anyway, we accepted liability, otherwise we'd still be in the Argentine.'

I was not travelling back on the boat with Gerry and the animals, but had arranged to fly from London Airport that evening to be at the zoo the next morning when the Ark arrived. Sophie left us and went to spend a week's well-earned rest at her home in Bournemouth. In the rush to get away from the docks I had not really had a chance to examine the collection properly, but Durrell told me about it on our way to Waterloo and we spent the rest of our journey exchanging news of ourselves and our various friends on both sides of the world.

At Waterloo Station we supervised the removal of the animals and baggage to the train, and then spent the remaining time with the friends who had come to see Gerry off.

The next morning I waited for them at the zoo. Durrell was so excited by everything that he did not know what to do first : look round the grounds or supervise the release of his collection into their various cages. Anyway, the staff

E

soon had everything out of their travelling boxes and into paddocks or cages. Of course, the puma, ocelot and other small cats had to go into our quarantine station. As I had suspected, Durrell was slightly put out that his blueprints for the zoo's development had not been followed, but this was softened by his delight at having all his African animals safely back with him again.

In our absence my pet squirrel Small had picked up a strange virus and died. I felt guilty at having left her, but then animals, like human beings, can catch diseases and die however carefully they are looked after—a thing that a lot of zoo goers seem to forget.

Instead of having animals in my bed, I now had them in the living-room, and at one time there seemed to be a constant procession; a sick peccary, Cholmondeley the chimpanzee with a slipped disc, a large Aldabra Tortoise with a mouth infection, Lulu the chimp with ear trouble, and various birds of which Dingle the chough was the most outstanding. He had been given to us by a lady in Dorset and was a most delightful character who enjoyed poking his beak into tea cups and investigating every nook and cranny in the room. We also had the occasional oiled gull, but perhaps the most distinguished of my visitors was N'pongo the gorilla. She was purchased on the H.P. plan— she had been offered to us by an animal dealer in Birmingham at the staggering figure of £1,500, money which we just did not have, but this did not daunt Durrell; he said, 'Yes, we'll have her,' and then set about trying to find the money. He rang all the wealthy people on the Island, asking them if they would care to own a piece of anthropoid ape, and whether it was his cheek or the unusualness of his request that appealed to some of these unsuspecting folk we will never know, but very soon we had raised the amount and N'pongo spent her first two days at Jersey Zoo occupying our living-room. She took over the flat completely, and compared with a lot of human beings whom I have had the doubtful pleasure of entertaining, her manners were exemplary. The one martyr in our household to all this is our long-suffering boxer dog, Keeper, who tolerates everything with a deep sigh and a look that quite obviously means that nothing more can surprise him about either us or the ghastly things with which we insist on infesting the house.

Sophie's stay in the zoo was very short-lived; her mother became gravely ill and she had no alternative but to leave us and go to look after her. We were all sorry about her mother's illness, and even sorrier at having to lose Sophie who had become by now an essential part of our family group. Our house was never quite the same without her, and after trying to cope with a stream of eager young women aspiring to be secretary to a famous author[1] it soon became more than obvious that we could never replace her. As I struggled manfully to answer all the fan letters, I looked back longingly on the days when Sophie would quietly take them all away and deal with them.

As our coffers were, as usual, nearly bare, Durrell finally got round to writing a book, and, after a tremendous struggle on my part, actually finished *A Zoo in my Luggage*, which dealt with our visit to the Fon of Bafut, and our arrival in Jersey.

It was now obvious to Gerry that more capital would be needed if the zoo was to progress at all. We were still a relatively unknown venture, especially to the holiday-makers, and so it was decided that we should approach the bank with a view to increasing our present loan by another £10,000, bringing our total indebtedness to £20,000 in all—a formidable sum. Hart-Davis again came to our rescue by offering to guarantee the further £10,000. All this appalled me, as I hate even buying an egg-timer on H.P., and I used to lie awake at nights, worrying about how it was all going to be repaid. I could not see the zoo ever being in a position to do so, and that would mean that we

[1] I hope that all the eager young women who might swim into my ken will bear this pungent sentence in mind. This also applies, of course, to the eager young woman who is typing this manuscript. G.D.

would be entirely responsible, for it had been agreed from the very beginning that our position in the zoo should be purely honorary, and that in return we should merely be supplied with a flat to live in. Many of our friends thought that we were quite mad but Durrell felt strongly that the zoo should not have the additional burden of paying us a salary. All that he asked of it was that it should be solvent and self-supporting; he would not interfere with its administration but would concentrate all his efforts on his own work which would, in turn, advertise the zoo and its aims.

During this period Gerry followed *A Zoo in my Luggage* with a second book, *The Whispering Land,* which was about our trip to the Argentine. These were followed by a series of articles for *The Observer*; a weekly page for a children's magazine; two children's books which were commissioned: *Island Zoo* in collaboration with that wonderful photographer Suschitsky, and *Look at Zoos,* a young person's guide to zoo going. All this, apart from radio talks and appearance on B.B.C. television, was no mean output by any standards.

I added to poor Durrell's worries by having myself carted off to a nursing home and losing half my innards as a result. His mother later told me that he suffered far more from the worry than I obviously did in actually having the operation.[2] When I left the nursing home after ten days he insisted upon playing nursemaid for another five weeks, and I got to the point where I was not at all eager to relinquish my privileged status as an invalid; I had a wonderful time, being waited on hand and foot with nothing to do all day but read or play records while my ever-loving husband attended to everything. I can recommend it as a profession—being an invalid, I mean.[3]

We then made our second major essay into television when one of the B.B.C. television producers, who is a close friend of ours, asked Gerry to do a series for children

[2] Remiss of me. I had still not checked on the assurance policy. G.D.
[3] For any wives who attempt to believe this statement I can only say that the quickest way to divorce is via the bedpan. G.D.

about the various animal families. This needed a lot of planning and also meant that a large number of live animals would have to be shown in the studio. How could we show these creatures without wire or bars or glass? Durrell loves problems of this kind and was soon fully immersed in the planning and preparation of the series, which was to be called 'Zoo Packet'. It was organised like a military operation, and the people in Bristol did everything we asked, even to laying on an entire British United Airways car ferry to transport our Land-Rover, packed to the gills with animals, plus another lot of cages. These were all flown to Bournemouth and then carried in B.B.C. vans by road to the Bristol Television Studios, where the programmes were to be recorded. The largest dressing-room was set aside as an animal house, while the No. 1 studio was arranged with stands and weird constructions on which the animals were to go. Although it was a most exhausting experience for all of us, I do not think that there was anyone who would have missed it.[4] Never before have eleven representatives of the primate family been shown live, together, in a television studio, and judging by what happened, never again will they be allowed to do so. It required everyone's ingenuity to keep these creatures occupied and prevent them climbing down on to the floor or disappearing into the rigging high in the studio ceiling, but somehow everyone coped magnificently. N'pongo, the young gorilla, had a dressing-room all to herself, and she behaved beautifully as always and seemed to appreciate fully the importance of the occasion. Unlike Sarah Huggersack, the giant anteater, she was not in the slightest bit temperamental and accepted everything as though it were perfectly normal. The series was again rather off-beat and unusual, and again received a mixed response.[5] But it was obvious from the many letters that we received that most people had enjoyed it and found it informative and inter-

[4] There was one : me. G.D.
[5] It was received with more than mixed feelings by the animals that took part in it. G.D.

esting, although one irate gentleman protested vigorously, saying that he was certainly not related to any monkey and how dare we suggest it.

We are often asked whether we answer all the letters that we get from readers and viewers. As our life depends on the good-will of the public who buy the books or watch us on television, it would be frankly very foolish, as well as very rude, not to answer all the letters that we receive, even though some of them are difficult. The abusive ones we try to deal with as carefully and good-naturedly as we can, but the odd twisted, unsigned letters we consign to the fire where they belong. Because of the books we have made many friends throughout the world. Many of these friends send us delightful Christmas cards every year, and we are often able to meet them if we visit their countries.

It was two years since Gerry had returned from the Argentine and we both felt that it was about time he explored new ground. It might also be possible, if we chose somewhere really interesting, to persuade the B.B.C. into coming with us on the trip, thus saving us all the heartache of doing our own filming. For weeks we pored over the atlas : India—no, far too late to make any of the elaborate arrangements that would be necessary; East and Central Africa—grossly overshot, filmically, and certainly would not tempt the B.B.C. This kind of thing went on for weeks until we happened to be over in London on business. I was wallowing in the bath of our hotel, thinking about the problem, when, like a flash, it came to me. I leapt out of the water, wrapped myself in the huge towel and rushed into the bedroom screaming, 'Gerry, I've got it! It's perfect and completely different from anything you've ever done before.'

'Hang on a minute and calm down and tell me quietly. I'm receptive to any ideas you have, if it means we're going somewhere interesting.'

'Well, first, are you dead set on it being a straightforward collecting trip?'

'No, not really, if you can think of a better idea that'll give me book material and a television series.'

'Fine. So how about going on a trip to New Zealand, Australia and Malaya, and studying at first hand their conservation efforts? You'll not only get a book and a possible series for television out of it, but you'll be able to see for yourself what's actually being done or not being done in these three countries. Apart from this, you'll also meet all the people who are concerned with the problem of conservation in these areas, and if you like we could even call in at East Africa on the way back and see all those parks too, though I don't suppose that filming there would appeal to the dear B.B.C. much, as they have lots of stuff from that area. Well, what do you think, Durrell?'

'Well, it's a good idea certainly, but I don't know if it's even possible. Let's first ring up Mr. Miles at Grindlays Bank and ask him to find out about boats for us. If we can work it in that way, then it's worth pursuing.'

Mr. Miles of Grindlays had suffered much at our hands in the past, but as usual did not seem at all put out by our suggestion.

'I think it perfectly possible, Mr. Durrell, and how long would you like to be in each country?'

'Oh, about six or seven weeks.'

'Well, you leave it to me and I will let you know within the next few days.'

The next obstacle to tackle was the B.B.C. Film Unit in Bristol. One of the poor unfortunate producers who happens to be a friend of ours is Christopher Parsons, and he was very intrigued by the idea.

Thus the scheme began to gather momentum, and soon we were dashing up and down the Strand, seeing people at Australia, New Zealand and Malaya House, who all helpfully provided us with the names and addresses of the Government Agencies we should approach. Chris's immediate boss was interested in our scheme but wanted a few more details before committing himself, so Chris flew over to Jersey[6] and between us we produced a very detailed memorandum which obviously satisfied not only the head of Western Region, but also the powers that be in London. There was a slight snag in that the B.B.C. party could not leave before April because of other commitments, so we changed our dates and agreed to meet in New Zealand on 5th April.

Rovers once again promised to help us, and to arrange a vehicle wherever and whenever we needed it. The B.B.C. took it upon themselves to lay on the Customs in every country, for which I, for one, was eternally grateful, and between us we wrote letters to all the important people in the three territories—all of whom replied enthusiastically offering to do everything they could to further our trip.

The Governor of Jersey at that time was the late Sir George Erskine who, with his wife, had always taken a close interest in both the zoo and us, and when he heard about our forthcoming trip he offered to give us letters of introduction to all the people he knew in each of these countries. His letter to Lord Cobham, the then Governor-General of New Zealand, proved to be the greatest asset, for Lord Cobham immediately approached the New Zealand Government and so brought into being the staggeringly efficient machine which was to open the entire country to us, and for this we will remain in his debt.

Armed with all our letters and nine suitcases (for we had to have a great variety of clothing on this trip), we left Jersey on a typical February day, with snow falling gently from the sky. From Rotterdam and the wintry weather of Northern Europe we turned southwards towards the warmth of the southern hemisphere, stopping only at Genoa and Aden before we reached Auckland on 4th April. It was a wonderful trip, but we could not wait to attack New Zealand.

---

[6] He does this at the drop of a hat to the detriment of my wine cellar. G.D.

CHAPTER 8

Our reception in Auckland was the most fantastic thing we had ever experienced. Waiting for us on the quayside we found not only the Government, represented by Brian Bell of the Internal Affairs Department, but the local representative of our publishers, Hart-Davis, and, perhaps the biggest surprise of the lot, two of Gerry's fans, Mr. and Mrs. Phil Warren who, with their two children, had come all the way into the city from their farm just to welcome us to New Zealand. We had corresponded with these two people for quite a long time, but were nevertheless deeply touched by this first sample of the overwhelming interest and kindness that was shown to us throughout our entire New Zealand tour.

'It's like a Royal Tour,' Gerry observed.

From the word go we were completely taken over by the Wildlife Department, for which we were eternally grateful, and Brian Bell was assigned to us during our entire stay and acted throughout as guide and mentor. He had already collected our Land-Rover from Wellington and he soon organised the Customs and the crew to act as porters. There is a strange attitude to service in New Zealand. Since everyone considers himself as good as everyone else, a theory with which I have no quarrel, no one willingly takes a job in which they have to serve others, for they seem to consider it beneath them. This attitude was to colour our impression of the whole country.

Soon the Land-Rover was bulging with all our baggage and film equipment, and as we drove into the city itself Brian outlined our programme for the next six weeks.

'Chris Parsons and Jim Saunders the cameramen have arrived in Wellington and we've laid on a car for them which will bring them up to meet you in Hamilton the day after tomorrow. We thought that you would both like twenty-four hours to get yourselves orientated before actually starting filming. Then there is a large lake near Hamilton where Black Swans are in absolute abundance, and we thought you might like to see this and film it. After that we go to Rotorua and then on to Wellington.'

Both Durrell and I were beginning to feel a little breathless and begged him to stop. By this time we were outside our luxurious looking hotel where a press reception had been laid on by a delightful character called Terry Eagen, the Government Press Officer. Reporters interrogated us gently and photographers popped at us as we talked and discussed our plans. This is where Brian Bell really came into his own; from what we could hear him say, every minute of our visit was planned for, and we would certainly see both New Zealand and its wildlife or Brian Bell would want to know why. In fact he became a much loved member of our team and it was entirely due to him that we got such wonderful films.

The rest of that day was spent dodging the Press, except for a brief interlude during which Durrell had the doubtful pleasure of sampling the joys of a New Zealand pub and the famous six o'clock swill.[1]

As a preliminary introduction to New Zealand wildlife, Terry Eagen suggested that we might like to see a colony of rare plovers called Wrybills not far away from Auckland, and it was only Durrell's consuming passion for natural history that forced him off his beery bed to drive several miles to see these charming little creatures. They were tiny grey birds with a curved beak, and they hopped about in a group, each standing on one leg, looking rather like ping-pong balls in a fountain. Having whetted our appetites to see more, we returned to Auckland to gather our wits and our voluminous baggage, and set off for Hamilton to begin our work.

Our reunion with Chris and Jim Saunders took place in a tea shop miles from anywhere. The local Wildlife Associa-

[1] Never again. G.D.

tion had laid on this part of our trip and we were also introduced to the members, who had all turned out to welcome us. Henry Arnfield, an Englishman who had emigrated many years ago, was assigned to our party, and thanks to him and his very efficient boat we were able to zoom around the lake and film the thousands of Black Swans that lived and bred there. These birds had been introduced into New Zealand by the early settlers, and like other introduced species had now reached pest proportions. As a result, the Wildlife Division had had to organise shoots to keep these birds under some sort of control. As Henry explained, no one wanted to wipe out the birds completely, but unless they were rigidly controlled they would leave no areas free for the native wildfowl, and a balance had to be enforced.

It was a very pleasant afternoon and we got lots of interesting film and sound recordings. During a break for the inevitable cup of tea, we discussed Brian's plans for us. It all sounded quite perfect, but depended entirely on the weather, especially for the off-shore islands. We also had a deadline to meet as we were due to sail for Australia on 5th May. Brian was optimistic about the weather.

'Well, when we're marooned in the middle of Cook Strait I'll remind you of this conversation,' said Chris plaintively. Brian laughed.

'No, I'm lucky and I can almost guarantee the weather.'

'Anyway, it's a bloody marvellous programme and I guarantee that we're going to have too much material if we're not careful, Christopher,' interrupted Durrell.

'I won't worry about that, Durrell. After all, I can always do three programmes on New Zealand if the material is strong enough.'

When we had finished filming Black Swans, we pushed on to Rotorua, the town world-famous for its geysers and mud pools and also its sulphur smell.[2]

We could smell Rotorua long before we actually saw it

[2] The smell was vaguely reminiscent of an obscure English railway hotel at lunch time. G.D.

and I began to wonder how its inhabitants could bear living with a smell of rotten eggs permanently in the atmosphere. Apart from this, Brian told us that it was a dangerous place to live in for you never knew when the earth would suddenly crack open and belch forth steam or gas. To underline this, he told us about a man who had recently completed fitting out a new shop, only to have the whole front blown in by escaping gas. As we drove down the main street, we could see steam rising from the main geyser area at the end of it and the smell became even more overpowering as we got closer.

'Shots of this will help build up the picture of New Zealand very well. After all, most people in Britain haven't got a clue what this country looks like, you know, and it's important to establish the area,' announced Chris.

In the good cause of television we descended into the small valley which housed the boiling water streams, hot geysers and bubbling mud pools. Slap in the middle of filming a sound take, the biggest geyser blew her top and covered both us and all our equipment with a fine spray of eggy water, nearly carrying poor Durrell off as he was standing right near the blow-hole. He got no sympathy from us as we had warned him not to go too close.

'It's all right for you lot to laugh your heads off, but I might have been damaged for life,' he muttered, wiping himself down.

'Never mind then, Gerry, it made a wonderful sequence, and will be a riot with the viewers,' Jim assured him.

The whole area was uncanny and reminded me of the 'Rite of Spring' sequence in Walt Disney's *Fantasia* which showed the Creation of the World. The mud pools themselves looked rather like toffee vats glugging away, and I could hardly tear myself away from them.

'Well, come on, you chaps, we've got to move on and film some wildlife, you know. This is not a travelogue in glorious Technicolor,' chivvied Chris.

'He's getting just like Nagger Bell here, isn't he, Jim? Never a moment's respite.' This was all that Jim needed

'When do we get a day off, Chris? Must catch up on the old sleep, you know, all work and all that.' Chris hastily side-stepped this one and turned to Brian to enquire where his friends from the Wildlife Department were who were going to show us the forestry problem.

'They're meeting us at the hotel after lunch and then we can decide what to do first, although it does look like rain.'

'Who cares about the rain? You don't mind getting drenched in the cause of television, do you, Jim?'

'No, it's not my camera after all, Gerry, and it's Chris who'll get the blame if we don't get the series, so why should we worry?' Poor old Chris was always the butt, though he took it all with great spirit and was soon hardened to anything we might say to him.[3]

After lunch Alan Hall, the local Wildlife man came to see us, and we spent the rest of that day filming on Lake Rotorua and visiting a trout farm.

Early the following morning we drove off with a forestry man to their research station in the centre of the vast pine plantation, where we met other forestry officers and scientists who were studying the problem of how to control opossum and deer. These introduced creatures were now rampaging throughout the whole of New Zealand, ruining its forests and causing erosion.

We drove along the well-defined forest roads in something like a funeral cortège, stopping occasionally to examine trees and undergrowth, and when we came to a heavily damaged area we persuaded one of the forestry officers to be interviewed and filmed. After this some of our escort left us, presumably alarmed that they too might be forced to stand in front of the dreaded camera. We drove on through the tall plantations to a fire observation tower in the heart of the forest area, which was run by a charming soft-spoken man who spent every summer here working as a fire warden with only his dog as a companion. The view from his eyrie was magnificent, and in the distance we could make out Mount Egmont, a volcano now believed to be extinct.

[3] *Almost* everything that was said to him. G.D.

Later we learned that this man was one of New Zealand's leading novelists who, wanting peace to write, had found himself the ideal job. Thus New Zealand was benefiting both ways.

By the time we returned to our hotel we were all pretty exhausted, and since, to Jim's horror, we had to leave for Wellington at five o'clock the next morning, we decided to go to bed early. Jim Saunders loved his sleep and could not function properly unless he had at least eight hours,[4] as he kept pointing out to Chris, without apparently much success.

'You can relax in Wellington, Jim,' he promised, but Jim was beginning to fear otherwise, as the pace we were setting was beginning to tell even on poor old Nagger Bell, the really tough one of the group.

'We've an awful lot of ground to cover, you know, before 5th May.'

'Yes, Chris,' we all bellowed in unison, 'but we want to have the energy to stagger on to the boat at the end of it all, and at this rate not even you are going to make it.'

Now the Grand Hotel in Rotorua is an old-established place where Royalty always stays on their tours[5] so it is not used to having five people struggling madly with baggage and equipment in its hallowed corridors at 4.30 in the morning.

Thanks to the dearth of porters we strained many a tendon and twisted many a muscle lifting our baggage around during our six weeks' stay. However, to offset this unfortunate situation some hotels have luggage trolleys for the guests. This is somewhat complicated by having lifts with automatically closing doors, so that just as you are ready to push your groaning trolley through the doors, they close smartly; thus it was that Durrell and Parsons ended up laughing hysterically in a large noisy heap under the

---

[4] The fact that he functioned inadequately even with eight hours' sleep is, I suppose, neither here nor there. G.D.

[5] One of the many and probably one of the most forceful reasons for not wishing to be Royalty. G.D.

baggage on the lift floor of the Grand Hotel. Somehow I don't think that it was sorry to lose this lot of distinguished guests.

The journey to 'windy' Wellington, capital of the dominion, was a hair-raising one. A violent storm pursued us all the way to the outskirts of the city, making us long to reach our luxurious hotel. We were doomed to disappointment. Again, there was no one to help with the luggage, and it was impossible to get anything to eat or drink before dinner was served at a quarter to six. Room service as such was left to the discretion of the floor maid who might, if provoked in the right way,[6] produce a cup of tea in the morning. From Wellington it was planned that we should make several sorties. Also we were to visit the heads of all the departments concerned with our trip, and Durrell was to have lunch with the entire New Zealand Cabinet, so there was not much time to be lost if we were to fulfil all our engagements, socially or otherwise.

Kapiti was a large island just off the coast, which had been made a bird sanctuary, and here George Fox and his wife watched over their charges most efficiently. Fox himself met us early one morning in his launch and ferried us the short distance across to the island. Kapiti was thickly wooded and apparently swarming with birds, but the stars of this sanctuary were the Kakas which were very tame and came whenever either George or his wife called them. It was a remarkable sight to see these large parrots circling around the house, lower and lower as George called them by their pet names, until they eventually came to rest on the bird table and from there to sit on George's head and eat the titbits that he offered them. They were not in the least worried by the humans or the cameras, and Durrell was nearly scalped by one that flew on to his head. Chris was delighted.

'Don't move him off, Durrell, it's a marvellous shot.'

'Thank you,' said Durrell, 'but will you pay for the injuries?'

[6] If provoked in the wrong way, almost anything could happen. G.D.

Chris's only rejoinder was to assure him that it was jolly good for the public image. These birds were natural comedians, as indeed all the bigger New Zealand parrots seemed to be, and they squabbled with each other and played tug-o'-war with pieces of date, almost overbalancing in their efforts to get more than their fair share. Finally they had had enough and disappeared as rapidly as they had come; soon all that was left was their harsh cries on the air, but Chris was overjoyed.

'That was wonderful stuff, Durrell, and I'm very grateful to you, Mr. Fox, for allowing us to come here and disturb you like this.'

George Fox looked slightly embarrassed at being thanked so effusively.

'It's nothing. Glad to help you, and you're always welcome.'

Brian later assured us that this was indeed praise, for apparently the Foxes didn't take kindly to eager ornithologists from overseas, and usually made no bones about it.

'Well, we can all sleep peacefully tonight,' cracked Jim as we drove back into the city. 'Chris is very pleased with himself today, so, who knows, we may be allowed out tonight for a few minutes.'

The next excursion was to Mount Bruce, and Durrell could hardly contain himself on the journey.

'To think that I'm at last going to see a real live Notornis; I never believed I would.'

The reason for this enthusiasm was because these birds had been thought to be extinct, but had been rediscovered in South Island in 1948. The Wildlife Department, in an attempt to preserve them, had decided to take a few young birds into captivity where they hoped they would breed and thus provide the nucleus of a thriving colony. This is what we were now on our way to see. They live in a large paddock immediately behind the game warden's house. He was just about to feed them, so we had arrived at exactly the right time. There was a tremendous commotion in the bushes and then what looked like a rugger scrum came into view, and from this the heavenly looking birds eventually disentangled themselves. About the size of a small turkey, with iridescent blue feathering and brilliant sealing-wax red legs and beaks, these fabulous birds emerged, looking almost as if they had stepped out of one of the *Alice* books. Their whole attention was riveted on the food pots, and they completely disregarded all of us until I offered one of them a banana. This held their attention and enabled Jim, Chris and Durrell to line up their cine cameras. Durrell was in raptures and could not stop talking and marvelling at their personality; they were certainly more than just decorative. Soon they were squabbling madly over the food dishes, and, carried away by Durrell's enthusiasm, Chris filmed them from every possible angle, running, walking, sitting, fighting, eating, the lot; he was determined not to miss a thing.

At last he was satisfied, and there remained one other thing for Durrell to drool over, a Kakapo, the largest New Zealand nocturnal parrot, which was almost certainly extinct in the wild state. Here again the Wildlife Department had tried to establish them in captivity, but unfortunately one of the pair died soon after being brought to the sanctuary, and the sole survivor was cherished by the warden. Because of its timidity, Durrell went alone to take a brief look at this remarkable bird sitting in its nest burrow.

It was a very elated party that returned at full speed to Wellington; everyone was satisfied with the day's activities.

We chose, with our usual foresight, to travel across to Picton in South Island by the overnight ferry boat at the height of the Easter holiday. It was only through the good offices of the New Zealand Government that we managed to get any accommodation at all, for the decks were jammed with human bodies, all clutching boots and rucksacks, the badge of office, apparently, of every New Zealander. As we had a luxury cabin—at least that is what it called itself, though death-watch had obviously set in—we swiftly installed ourselves in it and rang the service bell. After about half an hour, when nothing had happened, we tried again.

'I did warn you, Gerry, that things were a bit difficult on this ship, especially as it's Easter,' said Brian.

'Let's go and find a steward, if there is such a thing, and try and get some soda to weaken our Scotch with,' suggested Durrell. So they disappeared while Jim and I sat patiently in state in the faded splendour. Eventually they returned, triumphantly brandishing six sodas.

'What a bloody ship this is. Everything closed, and it was only by bribery and corruption that we managed to get these,' moaned Durrell.

Feeling rather more cheerful after an initial drink, we were still not prepared for the sudden intrusion of a fugitive from a woman's hockey team. This female inquired rudely who exactly was sleeping in the cabin. Rather timidly we said that we were, and that yes, we would like tea in the morning if that was humanly possible. Apparently satisfied, the apparition withdrew itself.

'What on earth was that?' exploded Durrell.

'That,' gurgled Brian, 'was your cabin stewardess.'

'It looked more like a wardress from a concentration camp to me. It's charming the way you New Zealanders go out of your way to make people welcome. All this friendly, courteous service constantly at your beck and call. Quite delightful.'

We went on in this vein until poor Brian begged us to stop.

At around 6.30 the next morning a cup of revolting tea was reluctantly hurled at us, promptly followed by Chris, Jim and Brian, all of whom had been turned out of their cabins as the stewards wanted to clean them out. We had arrived at Picton.

It was a beautiful morning, all mist and rosy pink, and even the old cattle boat looked picturesque in that light. A nearby café provided us with an excellent breakfast while we waited for the arrival of the launch which was to take us out into Cook Strait to the Brothers Islands. Jim and I were not looking forward to this trip for on top of the hideous sea journey (we are neither of us good sailors) there was only one way to get on to this island : in a pig net. One was hauled up by crane by the lighthouse keepers, twirling perilously over the sea and the rocks below. We felt that there must be an easier way to film animals, but anyway there was no escaping now. Quite a lot of people turned up to see us off as the local press kept everyone informed of our movements and interviewed us at every town.

Our trip along Queen Charlotte Sound was lovely for the sea was very calm and we all lay on the deck in the warm sunshine watching Cook Strait Blue Penguins swimming and diving all around us and a lot of other sea-birds skimming over the water. At the entrance to the Sound there are some jagged rocks which are the last refuge of the King Shags, large Cormorant-like birds which are persecuted by the local fishermen who wrongly insist that they affect their fishing.

'Perhaps we could film them on the way back, Chris. After all it would make a good sequence and is a good conservation story,' suggested Durrell.

'Yes, if we can get on to the rocks easily, let's do it by all means. I'm all for anything that keeps the theme strong. Is it easy, Brian?'

'I should think so, if the boatman is willing and the weather is good. I'll ask him.'

Soon the Brothers Islands loomed ahead and we could see the two lighthouse keepers walking down to the crane which would bring us aboard. Jim and I commiserated solemnly with each other, convinced that neither of us would survive the hazards of being hauled up by the fragile looking crane hovering above us.

'Jim, can you go up first with the cameras, and try to take some shots as you're lifted up? This'll give the viewers an idea of what it's all about.'

Valiantly he agreed to do this and was soon swaying madly above us. Chris was the next one, then Gerry and I

swayed in the large pig net together, and with eyes tightly
closed we were lifted aloft. It was the most terrifying
experience, and a tremendous relief to be dumped down on
the crane platform. I hurriedly scrambled out of the net
before someone whipped it out over the sea again. Our three
hosts, one north-country man and two New Zealanders,
welcomed us with varying degrees of enthusiasm. Bill
Wright, who as well as being a lighthouse keeper was
tremendously keen on natural history, turned to Brian.

'I got your message, Brian, and have caught a few
Tuataras for filming close up. Would you like to see them?'
he asked Gerry. What a question to ask Durrell!

These lizards have come down to us entirely unchanged
from the days of the great reptiles, and still possess the
remnants of a third eye in the centre of their foreheads.
Fortunately, they are found on various islands off the New
Zealand coast, and like all the New Zealand fauna are
strictly protected, although the authorities do not really
consider them to be in danger of extinction.

Bill Wright took us over to a small shed and opened the
door. The floor was a seething mass of Tuataras, but looking
like no zoo Tuataras we had ever seen. They were brightly
coloured with yellow frills along their backs and white
blotches all over their brown skins. Bill handed one to
Gerry who took it as if it was made of spun glass, but
the creature just lay in his hands and did not mind in
the least being examined so closely.

'Aren't they marvellous things, Chris?' Gerry enthused,
'and what lovely colours. You never see them like this in
zoos, and I'm beginning to think that it's because they're
kept too hot. If I manage to get a pair next year, I'm going
to build them a special house where I'll try to reconstruct
their natural habitat and control the temperature, and
I'm sure they'll do well.'

Soon he and Bill Wright were in deep conversation about
the problems of keeping Tuataras healthy, and this would
presumably have gone on all day if Chris had not reminded
them both that we were really there to film these creatures.

'Leave your discussion until tonight when the light's gone,' advised our producer.

The Tuataras co-operated beautifully in the filming, as if they wanted to be seen at their best, and while we were on the Brothers, we also filmed the Blue Penguins who shared the island with the Tuataras. However, their charm was rather spoilt for us when they spent the entire night braying loudly under the floor of the hut where we all slept dormitory-fashion. Even Gerry got a little bored by this chorus.

There is nothing quite like having an enormous breakfast of coffee, bacon, eggs and beans and watching the sun rise. It gives you a warm glow of satisfaction, almost of smugness. The weather, however, had changed a great deal from the previous day and began to look very angry.

'I doubt if the launch will come for you today,' said Bill, shaking his head. 'They don't like this type of sea much.'

'So much for our schedule,' observed Chris almost accusingly.

The rest of the morning was spent anxiously scanning the sea until we saw the launch ploughing heavily through the waves. Jim groaned.

'I think I'm definitely going to need seasick pills today.'

The crane trip down to the bouncing deck was less nerve-racking than the trip up and we soon had ourselves installed in the small cabin and were tossing our way to the White Rocks.

'Can we still get on to the rocks, Brian?' enquired Gerry.

'Yes, the boatman's willing to try.'

Jim, Brian, Chris and Gerry were ferried over to the rocks in the small dinghy, while I had the doubtful privilege of remaining in the launch. Poor Jim was obviously feeling very sick, but he nevertheless climbed up the crumbling rocks and got some excellent film of the King Shags. When he got back to the boat he slowly subsided on the bench and fell fast asleep.

Inside Charlotte Sound itself, the sea was much calmer,

but I don't think any of us were sorry to get off the launch
on to firm ground once more. Brian later told us that the
boatman had confided to him that he would not have made
the trip in the first place if he had realised just how bad
it was outside. Small comfort to us.

Christchurch was our next landfall where we were to
see the forestry nurseries run by an ardent conservationist,
John Holloway. Here again we saw evidence of what deer
and opossums were doing to the countryside, but we could
not stay long, and found ourselves heading for Dunedin
and the Royal Albatross nesting site which was watched
over by another Wildlife official, Stan Sharpe.

The Royal Albatrosses are magnificent birds and the
lighthouse promontory is the only nesting site to be found on
the coast of New Zealand, so a strict watch is kept to see
that no one molests them in any way. We were lucky and
found one Albatross chick, looking slightly depressed about
life, sitting in the scraping that was apparently a nest as
far as albatrosses were concerned. While we were talking,
Stan suggested that we might like to film the Yellow-eyed
Penguins which were also his responsibility and nested
quite near the town. The Yellow-eyed Penguins have
been saved from complete annihilation by the swift action
of the Wildlife Department—a perfect example of how
sensible conservation measures can save a species—but
this could not have been done without the full co-
operation of the general public and the local farmers
who appointed themselves honorary protectors of the birds.
The nesting-site of these penguins was a charming bay just
outside the city itself, but remote enough to make the whole
scheme a practical one. Climbing down on to the beach
was fairly simple and we all spread out to look for the
birds.

Durrell finally caught one of these lovely creatures, with
its pale yellow head and bright yellow eyes. He examined
it closely while Jim filmed it from various angles, and
when it was eventually released it shot off up the slope
to hide in a burrow.

'A remarkably handsome bird for a penguin,' Durrell insisted, 'and what a tremendous achievement for the Department.'

Stan merely smiled, but nevertheless seemed pleased that we had appreciated his work.

Reluctantly we left the shy kindly man and made our way towards Lake Te Anau National Park. It was here that we hoped to both see and film wild Notornis, although the chances of even getting a fleeting glimpse of these timid birds was remote, and after installing me at the rather palatial Government Hotel on the side of the lake, the four men flew off into the valley in a small float-plane which was the only method of getting into the area, except by walking. I had declined to accompany them for various reasons, but mainly because I needed time to catch up with the many kind letters that we had received, and also to write thank you letters to the countless people who helped us during our trip—a vital part of any expedition's activities.

It rained heavily the whole time we were in the valley, and the mists hung low over the peaks. The only Notornis they saw was gone almost before they had time to register it. I had agreed to meet them in the jet boat on the other side of the lake, and as the weather was far too bad for the plane to go into the valley, they had to walk down the slippery wet beech-covered slopes clutching their cameras, camping equipment and film. It was a very damp and depressed party that eventually came out on to the lakeside. I had enjoyed my brief respite in spite of the letters, and was looking forward to moving on again, but all Chris could do was moan. They had not seen a Notornis, nor, much to everyone's astonishment, any Keas—the mountain parrots that were supposed to be so common that one practically fell over them.

'I absolutely refuse to leave New Zealand until we have filmed Keas,' Chris announced.

As we were by now anxious to get on to Australia, the unexplained passion that Chris had conceived for these 'clowns of the snowline' threatened to be inconvenient. Keas are general favourites except of sheep farmers who swear that they attack young sheep to eat their kidney fat. The fact that this has not been proved one way or the other is of little importance to the average sheep farmer who blithely shoots at Keas whenever they appear, but it does mean that the bird is not protected and might be in serious danger in certain areas.

'The only other place we can try for Keas is The Hermitage at Mount Cook, a bit farther north from here,' Brian told him.

As time was getting short we made a hair-raising dash to Mount Cook. Needless to say we did not see any, and poor Chris was almost demented. One of the chambermaids overheard this lamentation.

'You want to film Keas?' she enquired. 'Well, why didn't you tell me? They come here every morning to the kitchen window and we feed them titbits on the roof.'

'Oh, no. I can't believe it. All that rushing about and now she calmly tells me that they come on the roof outside our rooms every morning! It's too much.'

Sure enough the next morning four fat silly-looking green parrots were fighting and squabbling over bread and butter just below us. Jim loaded his camera and shot foot after foot of these ridiculous birds who refuse to take life seriously or behave in the dignified manner befitting a parrot. Instead, they tore around the hotel pecking at everything, tearing up cardboard boxes, trying to disembowel our Land-Rover and anything else they found.

'Can we leave now, Chris dear boy, and get on the boat for Australia?' we demanded.

'Yes, I'm perfectly happy, and I think we've got some damned good programmes out of this little lot.'

Our friends in the Wildlife Department threw an enormous party for us and it was with the greatest difficulty[7]

[7] Since good food outside private homes is apparently non-existent in New Zealand, is it small wonder that I was reluctant to be removed from an atmosphere redolent with good smells, good wine

that we prised Durrell away from it to finish packing. Jim decided to fly to Sydney and wait for us there, while we luxuriated in a de luxe cabin on a delightful old ship called the *Wanganella*, and spent five days working hard on the script for the next stage, Australia.

CHAPTER 9

The Master of the *Wanganella* insisted that we get up at dawn to see Sydney harbour, and I must say it was worth the effort.[1] Normally when natives of a country wax enthusiastic about the beauties of some particular area, I find it disappointing, but not in this case with the famous bridge glowing in the morning sunlight.

On the quayside Jim Saunders was waiting for us with the Australian representatives of Hart-Davis, the British Council and the B.B.C. The Customs couldn't have been nicer and we were driving through the vast pulsating city of Sydney almost before we realised it. Mercifully, Mr. Williams, of the British Council, had fixed a press interview for the afternoon in his offices, so we had a few hours to gather our wits. We were entertained to an extremely lavish lunch by the B.B.C. man, nearly running off with his car in the process. The poor man had offered to drive us down to the restaurant, but for some unknown reason we had taken it for granted that he was not coming with us, so

---

and convivial company. There are times, however, when my wife behaves like a particularly debased Presbyterian elder and does not see eye to eye with me on these things. I can only attribute it to her north-country upbringing. G.D.

[1] At the time I had to say that I thought the view was magnificent as I was hemmed in on all sides by large, hairy Australians, none of whom I trusted. In actual fact, I feel that even the gates of heaven, if you were forced to get up at dawn to view them, would be depressing to say the least. G.D.

while we all rode in his enormous car, he had to walk. Then we booked into our hotel which Chris announced was a temperance hotel.

'Whatever possessed you to go to a temperance stronghold?' demanded the stricken Durrell.

'It's very cheap.'

'But what about me and my longing for a quiet drink as the sun goes down?'

'Well,' said Jim, 'you could always smuggle it in, I suppose.'

'Oh yes, and chew peppermints afterwards to mask the smell.'

But we were nevertheless unprepared for the condition of entry into these holy portals : we all had to sign the pledge. Luckily, we were only going to be there for one night, so we agreed to consume vast quantities of liquor before we actually went back to the hotel.

The Land-Rover that was awaiting us was another violent shock to our systems.

'What on earth is that?' we chorused at Jim. He giggled.

'That's the Land-Rover that's going to take us around Australia.'

'But that thing will never get us anywhere; it looks ready for the scrap-heap.'

'Well, all I know,' wailed Jim, 'is that that was supplied to me at the Sydney garage and when I complained they told me to take it up with the main agency in Melbourne.'

It was a terrible old thing not merely past its first flush of youth, but teetering on the grave. However, we squeezed ourselves into the cabin and drove round to the hotel.

So began the most hectic twenty-four hours that I personally have ever known. The Press were anything but gentle this time and positively made us snarl. Added to this was an endless round of people that we 'just had to go and see'—at least that is what Chris said. He seemed to be under the impression that Sydney was a bad influence on us, for he could not wait to push us out and on to the road. Not that any of us got a chance to find out what Sydney was like.

His Mecca was Canberra, the Federal Capital and the headquarters of the C.S.I.R.O. (Commonwealth Scientific and Industrial Research Organisation) Wildlife Division, and he was determined to get us there as soon as he could. It was almost the last straw when, after arriving in Canberra at some unearthly hour, we found that there was not a hotel to be had—that is, apart from a flea-bitten, run down, Western-type saloon about five miles beyond the capital. The whole place had an air as if the Indians had just passed through; still, it was somewhere to sleep, I suppose.

On our way back into Canberra, Chris filled us in about the people we were to meet, and warned us that we might not have a very easy passage with the head of C.S.I.R.O., Harry Frith, whom he had met very briefly on his way through to New Zealand. Australians are rather like north-country people; there are no halfway measures, and they either like you or they don't.[2] If they do, they will move heaven and earth for you. This is an attitude that I found frankly refreshing after years of living in the south of England where people will do anything rather than tell you what they honestly think.[3] So, crossing our fingers, we entered Mr. Frith's office. Everything hinged upon this man's co-operation. He did not look exactly overjoyed to see us, but was quite polite and even asked us to sit down. This was not a man you could beat around the bush with, or who would relish your wasting his valuable time, so without further ado Chris and Durrell launched into their recital while Harry Frith just sat there, occasionally nodding

[2] If I may correct this erroneous image, I would like to put it on record that Australians bear absolutely no resemblance to north-country people—Australians are nice. G.D.

[3] My wife, in her innocence, does not realise that there is an extremely good reason for the prevarication of what she calls 'the southern butterflies'. If they really said what they honestly thought, she would probably never speak to them again. G.D.

his head and making a remark. At the end of it all he thought for a few seconds and then said,

'Look, I personally would like to help you if I can, but I can't make my boys stop their work and help you unless they personally feel they want to. Now, I have to go to a meeting in a few minutes but I'll take you out into the yards and you can meet some of them. Then if they say it's okay, fair do's.'

The yards were in fact large paddocks just behind the offices where marsupials such as kangaroos and echidnas were kept in a confined area so that they could be studied at close quarters. Harry Frith introduced us to several of the scientists who were mainly concerned with kangaroos. The whole problematical question of the kangaroo is being investigated extensively by scientists at this station, and the C.S.I.R.O. had the unenviable task of making a case either for or against the kangaroo. Perhaps the leading expert on marsupial reproduction is Dr. Geoff Sharman, and it was through this charming man's interest and enthusiasm and eager agreement to help us that we really got anything at all for our Australian programmes. During a further conversation that afternoon in Harry Frith's office, it was agreed that we should return to Canberra on 1st June in the hope of filming the actual birth of a kangaroo. This had never been recorded fully on film before, and Chris Parsons was beside himself with joy, for this would really make the climax to the whole series. In return for their help, Chris offered the C.S.I.R.O. a copy of any film that we might take.

Very well satisfied with himself, Chris cracked the whip again, and we soon found ourselves in Melbourne talking to Mr. Alfred Butcher, the head of the Wildlife Service for the State of Victoria. On the way down our very ancient Land-Rover had decided that she was not too keen on joining our expedition, and her rear differential had gone. Thanks to help from a local garage and a passing police car, we managed to return her to the Melbourne agent who agreed, albeit reluctantly, to supply us with a younger vehicle which might perhaps be a little more reliable.

In the meantime, Miss Ina Watson of the Wildlife Service had arranged for us to stay, to Durrell's delight, in a pub, and we spent several pleasant nights in this place, which was run by a north-country woman whose one ambition in life seemed to be to stuff us with as much food as we could possibly eat.

Our first sortie was to Sherbrooke Forest, a heavily wooded area not far from the centre of Melbourne itself. Here lyre birds entertained the visitors regularly by dancing on their mounds and imitating all the other birds in the forest. The star attraction of this small group of accommodating birds was called Spotty, and he soon appeared and graciously took the titbits that we offered him, but nothing would induce him to get on his mound and do his little dance for the cameras. Several very cold wet days were spent in pursuit of Spotty, but he still held firm. We met three extremely tame and tenacious kookaburras, and Gerry encountered a fat, rather weary wombat, who looked for all the world like Pooh Bear after a heavy honey session, but he soon scurried back to his burrow when he encountered Durrell's mud-encrusted boots. Chris was again full of despair, and Jim in desperation hared off into the forest clutching his camera, leaving us on duty at the mound with the other camera and the recording machine. About an hour later he reappeared, beaming and smiling.

'It's all right now, Chris,' he said, waving his hand. 'You don't have to worry any more; I've got it all. Not one male lyre bird dancing, but two! Another little Rembrandt.'

Chris could hardly believe this and he was not finally convinced until the film was developed and he actually saw it for himself.

'Bloody marvellous, Jim,' was all he could say; he was absolutely delighted and Jim was rightly very pleased with himself.

Koala bears could not possibly be left out of any pro-

gramme about Australia, although we were beginning to
wonder how we could put them in without departing from
our central theme, but here again Miss Watson came to
our rescue. Apparently the Victoria Wildlife Department
had for many years been responsible for the protection of
these cuddly creatures, and as a result the species which was
once threatened with extinction was now safe. But a further
problem has arisen; because of the increase in their
numbers they were apt to eat an area out of eucalyptus
trees, and since they are not very sensible creatures, they
failed to realise that they had to move on to a more lush
area. So the Department occasionally caught a small group
of bears and transported them to a new area, and this is
what we were going to see.

We were intrigued to know how the wardens were going
to catch these rotund bears. Anyone who has ever tried
to pick a bear up will realise that there is not a great deal
to grip hold of, and koalas have a particularly thick pelt.
However, some ingenious person had evolved a very simple
method which caused the minimum discomfort to the bears.
The drill is that you find a tree with your koala bears in it.
You then produce a very long tubular metal pole with a
slip noose attached to it. Now the bears are extremely
trusting creatures and make no effort to move when the
noose is put round their neck. Of course, it has a catch on
it to prevent the bear being strangled. While one person is
operating the noose the rest of the party collect underneath
the tree holding a round cover which acts as a catch net.
Then a sharp tug and the bear comes hurtling unharmed
into the waiting cloth. They are then skilfully and speedily
put into special collecting boxes. It all happens so swiftly
that the bears never quite realise what has happened to
them. We caught up about a dozen koalas of various sizes,
and although they look cuddly and inoffensive, Durrell
found to his cost, when trying to assist a rather overweight
bear up a tree, that they have extremely sharp front claws.
The biggest enemy of the dim-witted koala bear today is the
bush fire, for they merely cling to a tree until they are burnt

to a cinder. A horrible end for such a charming and harmless animal.

While in Victoria we were privileged to see yet another animal that had been rediscovered after being considered to be completely extinct. A tiny little marsupial, Leadbeater's Possum. There were two of these little animals in captivity at the Wildlife Department's headquarters in Melbourne, but we were anxious to see the small area in the Dandenongs where they still lived. The site of the habitat itself was a very well-guarded secret, but, being such a small area, it worried us lest a forest fire should wipe out the whole population. I never remember being so cold, even in an English winter, as I was during that cold autumn night as we prowled up and down the road listening for the sounds of Leadbeater's Possum moving softly through the trees. We all had powerful battery searchlights with us, and so it was easy to see any animal once it came into our beam. We saw many other types of opossum and gliders that night, and were beginning to despair of finding the Leadbeater's when our guide stood quite still, put his fingers up to his lips to warn us to be absolutely silent, and turned his powerful beam on a nearby tree; and there it was—a Leadbeater—sitting quite still on the branch and peering at us. To me it looked like a cross between a squirrel and a bush baby and did not seem to be in the least worried at being stared at by quite a crowd of human beings. Everyone forgot about being frozen. Then with a small squeak it disappeared up the tree.

'Well, it was worth it all, wasn't it, Chris?'

Chris was in no fit state to answer, and it was not until he was standing in the forest hut before a roaring fire, drinking hot tea heavily laced with Scotch that we got a word out of him.

'Very nice, very nice,' was all he would commit himself to saying. 'Make a jolly good story for the series.'

Back at the hotel we returned to a freezing room, and Gerry was so cold that he refused to take his clothes off before getting into his cold bed.

Our visit to Victoria ended with a trip to the Healesville Sanctuary, a place always to be associated with that great Australian naturalist, David Fleay, but then run by Bill Gasking and his wife. It poured with rain all day, but we got some excellent film of wombats, koalas and platypus, and we saw the magnificent lyre bird cage presented to the sanctuary by the R.A.C. Yet the thing that remained deep in my memory was the horrifying sight of a recent bush fire which had come so near to destroying the entire sanctuary. Despite valiant efforts by everyone concerned, several kangaroos had been badly burnt on their feet and it was only with skilled and devoted attention that they recovered. In Europe we often hear about the bush fires in Australia, but it is not until one actually sees the maimed trees and dead animals that it really impinges upon you just how horrible these things are, and the tragedy is that most of them are started through carelessness on the part of some thoughtless individual. The suffering to both humans and animals cannot be measured, and it is little wonder that the penalties for starting a fire are so high.

Somehow we managed to keep our date in Canberra with Geoff Sharman and his pregnant kangaroo, Pamela, but she decided that she was not yet ready, so we removed ourselves to a luxurious motel down the road and kept vigil. It was almost like having a baby ourselves, and at every move she made we rushed hopefully over to the cameras. For two days she dragged it out, and the boys spent one whole night standing by their cameras. I think everyone in Canberra knew that we were waiting for this baby, for our toing and froing was in the fine tradition of the Keystone Cops. Needless to say we were back at the motel when she finally started in earnest. Never has a camera crew scrambled with such speed. Up at the yards, Pamela had chosen a comfortable corner and was leaning against the fence, carefully cleaning out her pouch. Almost before we realised it the baby was born, and we watched the minute thing crawl painstakingly up and up its mother's stomach until it finally reached the pouch, where it fastened on to one of the teats. It seemed incredible that this blind, almost embryonic joey should manage to find its way through that mountain of fur without any help at all from its mother. She was totally unconcerned with her new offspring, and bent only on cleaning herself up.

The birth had been taken on both cameras and everyone was pleased that it had gone so well. Boswell, who has since grown into a handsome grey kangaroo, made television history. It was the very first time that a kangaroo birth had ever been shown to the general public.

To show us the other side of their kangaroo survey, Harry Frith and his assistant, Bevan Brown, took us to a large sheep station outside the small town of Griffith. This belonged to a friend of Harry's who was helping the C.S.I.R.O. with their kangaroo control work. As we drove along the dirt road, we saw big red and grey kangaroos and emus everywhere, as well as the occasional fox. And overhead parakeets and cockatoos wheeled and called; the whole thing reminded me of the Argentine pampas. Harry and his team had constructed a special kangaroo trap so that they could mark the kangaroos with special collars and so check their range and movements. We spent a hair-raising hour touring over the country in Land-Rovers rounding them up for marking and checking.

Griffith itself was unique in New South Wales for it had set aside a piece of the Mallee Country as a permanent sanctuary for the Mallee Fowl. These are large, turkey-like birds which incubate their eggs in an earth oven which they construct themselves, regulating the temperature by putting on and removing soil as necessary. It was while driving along the road to the Mallee Fowl Sanctuary that we came upon a whole line of dead young Wedge-tailed Eagles crucified along a paddock fence. These wretched birds, like the New Zealand Kea, are persecuted by the sheep farmers, again because they are said to worry and kill young sheep.

Chris now decided that we ought to go up to Queensland and visit David Fleay. His animal sanctuary was at Burleigh

F

Heads, just over the Queensland border and very near Surfer's Paradise, a long stretch of golden beach beloved by the Australian holidaymakers. For years Gerry had told me about this dedicated man who had devoted his entire adult life to the cause of conservation in Australia, and had successfully kept and bred the Duck-billed Platypus in captivity.

It was obvious from the moment they met that Durrell and he were kindred spirits, and they were soon engrossed in the problems of wildlife and its survival all over the world.

Chris and I took this opportunity to go into Brisbane to get some money. Although it was autumn, the weather in Queensland was gorgeous and it was nice to be warm again after the bitter cold of Victoria and the chill winds of Canberra. Jim, sneaking away when Parsons's back was turned, spent the day on the beach and was apparently nearly eaten by sharks for his pains.

We spent a few fascinating days with David Fleay and his wife Ingrid, who seemed delighted to have us and show us their collection. The first thing we saw was the koala colony, and one tiny koala who strongly objected to being removed from his mother's pouch and rushed back inside the moment David released him. An Albino Emu conceived an overwhelming passion for Durrell and followed him around the paddock peering over his shoulder and looking adoringly up into his face. She even tried to persuade him to help incubate a clutch of eggs. But the character of the collection was a bossy young Cassowary called Claude who ruled the paddock with a well-aimed kick at any kangaroo who dared to get in his way.

The main charm of the Fleay collection lay in that all the animals were hand-tame and seemed to know David; even his Platypus (and male Platypus are notoriously difficult when handled) allowed himself to be picked up. In the basement of his house David kept a very fine reptile collection and also some of the smaller marsupials that he had bred. Fleay is one of the few people in Australia who,

despite a lot of opposition and indifference from the agricultural community, is really concerned for the rights of the
native fauna to exist side by side with the sheep and the
cattle.

It was sad when our filming came to an end, and we
left Chris and Jim to have a well-earned holiday while
we dashed back to Sydney to catch our boat to Singapore.
In Sydney the Press caught up with us again, and this
time we could really tell them how much we had enjoyed
both the country and its animals—which seemed to surprise
most of them.

Our arrival in Malaya was quite different from anything
we had experienced in either New Zealand or Australia.
We docked at Singapore to find that Chris and Jim had
dragged themselves away from the delights of the Great
Barrier Reef to join us. Chris actually allowed us to stay
for twenty-four hours in Singapore—a mixed blessing for it
was both hot and steamy and there was a water shortage.

Durrell was delighted to be back in the tropics and had
always wanted to go to Malaya, mainly I think because all
his friends who had been there had adored it. Driving
over the causeway into the Federation itself, we had
another little mishap with the Land-Rover and nearly
lost a wheel, but the British Army came to our rescue and
fixed it for us. We were due at a small reception the
British Press Office were giving in our honour in Kuala
Lumpur that afternoon, but halfway there we blew a
gasket and limped at about five and a half miles an hour
to the next small town where a Chinese garage proprietor
did a running repair. Even so, we did not reach the capital
until very late and missed the reception.

We had been accommodated in a luxurious air-
conditioned hotel called 'The Federal'. Each room had its
own bathroom, and the food was excellent—both Chinese
and European. Jim doggedly stuck to meat and two veg,
leaving the three of us to indulge our more exotic tastes.
Jim always seemed to be under the impression that there
was a conspiracy on the part of the local inhabitants to

poison him, and despite sticking to European food, it was
he alone who ended up with mild dysentery. The Federal
Hotel also seemed to be the main centre for all Chinese
social activity, so I very sportingly offered to sit with my
back to the room, enabling the three males to ogle every
Chinese female who came through the door.[4] I always
knew when some exotic creature had entered the room for
all conversation ceased and three heads and three sets of
staring eyes turned in her direction. European women are
at a decided disadvantage in a place like Malaya, and
probably throughout the Far East; the climate is against
them,[5] and so, most certainly, is the fragile grace of the
women. We once shared a lift with a most beautiful
Malay woman, and Jim and Chris were nearly bisected
by the closing lift doors in their eagerness to see which
floor she got out at. They were stunned when they saw
her next morning sharing the breakfast table with a ghastly-
looking European.

'What's he got that we haven't?' muttered Jim.

'Money?' I suggested.

Another thing about Kuala Lumpur that fascinated the
men was the numerous massage parlours which, we were
told, were merely a front for brothels. But no amount of
encouragement would persuade any of them to find out
definitely.[6]

Before reaching Malaya, we had warned Chris that
dealing with officials in tropical countries is quite different
from dealing with officials in temperate climates. He had
promised us that he would not develop ulcers or chew his
fingernails down to his elbows if things were not done
promptly, but after a week and a half had passed without
one foot of film going through the cameras, Chris was

[4] I have never ogled a female in my life. A wink, perhaps, or a
discreetly dropped wallet, but never an ogle. G.D.
[5] European women are at a disadvantage everywhere, including
Europe. G.D.
[6] A gross and damnable lie. G.D.

seriously contemplating suicide. However, things did then start to look up a bit and we decided to take ourselves to the Taman Negara, the National Park in the provinces of Kelantan, Pahang and Trengganu.

We drove along excellent roads to a small town called Kuala Lipis on the Jelai river, where the chief Game Warden, James Aw, had arranged for us to be met by jet boat and transported up the river to the 1,677 square miles of the National Park. Kuala Lipis itself was a reasonably sized community with very modern looking bank and cinema, and we stayed overnight in the rather ramshackle Rest House. Early the next morning the jet boat arrived and we were soon speeding up river at a phenomenal rate. Jim, who had purchased an army-type pull-on hat, was sitting in the bows with me when a sudden gust of wind removed this piece of military elegance from his head. He swore seriously that he would die of sunstroke, and we teasingly promised to buy him a topee, specially engraved—when we got back to Kuala Lumpur. A little later, rounding a bend in the river, we saw a small village perched high up on the river bank. Our driver decided to tie up and go and see somebody, and Jim, delighted, announced that he was going to buy himself a hat. In spite of our derisive roars of laughter, Jim set off up the bank, saying that he would bring us each back a nice iced drink. Much to our chagrin he appeared about ten minutes later, not only wearing a hat, but also clutching four bottles of iced Coca-Cola. Somewhere in this collection of mud huts he had found a tiny store boasting a kerosene refrigerator and an elegant selection of men's headgear.

Eventually the driver returned, and on we went, passing water buffalo browsing in the river and an odd collection of native huts. Shooting the rapids was a wonderful experience. These jet boats were originally developed in New Zealand and have such a shallow draught that they can get over anything. The only thing they are not equipped to cope with are the leaves floating on the surface of the water. These jam the propulsion mechanism, and our poor driver had to clamber over the side and submerge himself about four times in order to clean it.

It felt as if we had been travelling for hours, and in spite of the driver repeatedly saying, 'The Rest House is round the bend of the river,' we had begun to despair when, sure enough, we could see it in the distance. To add to it, the heavens opened at that moment and the rain fell down as only tropical rain can. Naturally, the equipment had to be protected and not us, so we sat and were drenched.

When we reached the landing stage, hordes of porters appeared to carry our baggage, while we tore up the steps and along the path to the main Rest House. To our horror, it was infested with a party of English school-children from Kuala Lumpur who had come to the National Park on a sort of gigantic nature ramble. In fact some of them turned out later to be knowledgeable and helpful both about the Park and the Federation.

Later, the head Game Warden of the Park invited us over to his house to discuss our plans. He was a charming old rogue, obviously petrified of his boss in Kuala Lumpur and over-anxious to help us. He arranged for one of his rangers to go with us into the jungle the next day and show us the various observation hides, and also promised to lend us whatever boats we needed to go up the river and explore some of the creeks. I don't know who was the more apprehensive, Jim or I. Neither of us liked the tropics and I always find tropical forests claustrophobic—quite apart from the leeches. We had all taken the precaution of equipping ourselves with jungle boots which would, theoretically at least, keep them off our feet and legs, but one could not go outside the Rest House compound without being attacked by an army. Durrell had two methods of dealing with them : one was a lighted cigarette and the other was salt; but most of the time they would manage to get in some hidden nook or crevice, to be discovered when we de-leeched ourselves back at the Rest House. Of all the things that infest tropical areas, I think these are the most revolting, and the most horrible thing about them is the amount of blood spilt in getting them off; you soon begin to look like walking wounded. On one trip I managed to get one on my leg, and since I was wearing tight jeans I had to disrobe completely to get it off—to the unsympathetic amusement of the men.

It was Jim who suffered again. This time through being closeted for hours on end in the stuffy hides in case the odd rhino happened to pass by. Luckily the gibbons relieved the monotony. They were everywhere in the trees above us, swinging gaily from tree to tree and calling to each other. The natives called them *wah wah* because of the noise they make, and to my mind they are quite the most delightful of the apes. In Kuala Lumpur we had met a Dutchman who had a black gibbon or siamang as a pet. The ape had the complete freedom of his house, and I honestly think that it meant more to him than even his own children. It was completely spoilt and rode around the city in its owner's car, honking madly.

While filming some river scenes and the large fruit bats that inhabit the forest, Chris and Durrell had landed on one of the sandbanks. They were crouching by the edge of the river, gazing into the water and discussing what to film next when they suddenly saw a large black cobra swimming towards them. They both kept very still until the cobra got within striking distance, when it suddenly saw the men, reared back in alarm, and tore off in the other direction. Chris was a bit shaken, naturally, but as Gerry said, this was another example of how much human beings terrify snakes. On the river bank we also saw the occasional Mouse Deer, a sweet little creature about the size of a small dog and much prized by the forest-dwellers for its meat, and occasionally we could see the red, highly coloured Rhinoceros Hornbill balanced precariously on the fragile branches at the top of some tree, or sweeping past. But the larger mammals eluded us completely, and this threw Chris once again into a deep depression.

Our next filming session was to take place on the eastern

coast of Malaya at the famous turtle beach at Dungun—
the only known site where the Giant Leathery Turtles lay
their eggs. Here the Malayan Nature Society had persuaded
the Government to help them establish a sanctuary, for year
after year these inoffensive giants had returned to the
beach, laboriously dug nest-holes in the soft golden sand,
and laid their large clutch of eggs, only to have them all
dug up again by the Malayans, and sold commercially.
Which meant that unless something was done to protect
these eggs, the turtles would die out entirely. So two years
previously a section of the beach had been set aside for the
turtles, and it was this that we were to see.

To get there we had to cross several big rivers on a sort
of pontoon ferry which looked precarious, and apparently
was, for one had sunk not very long before while ferrying
a bus full of people. Happily, nothing happened to us and
we eventually arrived at Dungun to be met by the Fisheries
Officer and his assistant. They in turn introduced us to
the Malay who held the egg concession, and it was through
him that we were allowed on to the protected section of
the beach. He explained that the turtle came up at night
and that it was essential not to disturb her until she had
actually started to lay her eggs, for once she had started
nothing would stop her, but if she was disturbed before she
reached this stage, she would leave and probably never
return.

We returned later that night with some powerful lights
lent to us by the Malayan authorities. Trudging along a
vast beach in the dark, your feet disappearing up to the
ankles in the soft clinging sand, and carrying weighty equipment in a temperature well over the eighties, is not my
idea of spending a warm tropical night. It seemed miles
before we eventually stopped.

'Come on, no time to sit around,' said Chris. 'We've got
to be ready to dash along the beach the moment we're
given the signal.'

'Yes, sir,' we all chanted in unison.

Patiently we waited for the summons, defending ourselves from the dive-bombing mosquitoes as best we could, and it seemed as usual that I was their favourite target.

'Quickly, quickly,' someone shouted, 'the turtles have come.' Staggering along the beach as quietly as possible we found the owner of the voice.

'She's just here,' he said. 'Now be very quiet until she starts to lay. Now!' he shouted, and there was a great blaze of light. When we had accustomed ourselves to the blinding glare we got our first glimpse of the Leathery Turtle. She was an enormous, ungainly creature struggling and panting in the heat and pouring a stream of what looked like ping-pong balls into the sandy cavity beneath her. Great globules of mucus streamed from her eyes with the effort. At last the flow of eggs stopped and she began to cover them with the loose sand that she had banked at either side of her. The powerful hind flippers quickly scooped it into the hole and at intervals she would stop to press it all down firmly with her great nine-foot body before adding more sand. At last, satisfied that her eggs were safe, the great reptile began her slow progress down the beach towards the pounding surf; this time using her front flippers to drag her huge carapace down and down the slope to the water's edge, leaving behind a trail like a tank track. When she arrived at the sea she flung her enormous head into the waves as if to cool and clean herself, then with one final push, launched her whole body into the waiting sea, and gave us a final wave with her flipper before disappearing into a dark wave.

Back at the nest site the eggs were being uncovered, this time not to be taken away and sold, but removed to a specially prepared site farther down the beach, which was enclosed behind wire-netting. In daylight it resembled a miniature military cemetery, for each little hole of eggs had a plain wooden cross above it on which was marked the date and number of eggs that had been buried. Several weeks later the most charming baby turtles dug their way up to the surface, looking for all the world as if they were dressed in natty pin stripes. They were collected up, placed

in a large water-filled container, and taken out to sea
by the Fisheries launch beyond the point where predators
normally waited to snap up unwary baby turtles. It is too
early yet to assess how successful these methods have been,
but at least it is a start and the turtles are being saved
from complete extinction.

Our producer was really getting into his stride now, and
pushed us even farther up-country; first to Ipoh to visit
an ornithologist, Geoffrey Alan, and his wife, who both
knew a great deal about the surrounding area and promised
to show us the Flying Lizard. They welcomed us warmly
to their home, and entertained us royally, and allowed us
to infest their garden with all kinds of equipment in an
effort to film the Flying Lizard. This creature looks dull
until you notice the fragile membranes attached to its
sides, which open like wings when the reptile launches
itself from one tree to another with effortless ease. There
is some doubt as to who was more relieved when this film
sequence was finished—the poor creature whom we pursued
hotly from tree to tree, or us, but we were not allowed
a break and soon Jim Saunders was photographing cicadas,
spiders, horned 'beetles and any other poor unfortunate
insect that happened to light in our area.

'It all helps to build up the picture,' insisted Chris.

Geoffrey Alan had foolishly told Chris that there was a
lot of interesting stuff to see farther up-country at Taiping
and Perak, but for once I was excused, and while the
three men went off in pursuit of more material, I stayed
behind in Ipoh with the Alans. Betty Alan and I soon
got on famously, and I went into the bush with her while
she took still photographs of various plants and shrubs
that she was particularly interested in. We had such a
good time doing nothing very much, that I was frankly
sorry when the men reappeared and whisked me off back
to the capital. We had been deeply touched by the kindness
and overwhelming hospitality that we had received in
Malaya, but I was nevertheless looking forward to going

on to East Africa and seeing once again the vast open grass plains.

Jim and Chris flew home and it seemed odd to be on our own again after so many weeks in their company; we both missed them a great deal. As for us, we suddenly changed our plans and decided to sail directly home when we heard that Gerry's mother was far from well and also received some disquieting reports about the zoo. East Africa would have to be left for another time. Through the good offices of the Shell Oil Company we got passages on a Glen Line ship, and I have never enjoyed a voyage so much, nor had as much fun as on that five week journey home. It was, of course, a tremendous relief not to have a collection of animals to look after, although we had managed to acquire three squirrels and four hanging parrots in Malaya, but these were quite simple to care for, compared with the problems we had had on our return from Africa and South America. The whole trip was like a wonderful holiday.

CHAPTER 10

We were welcomed back by Gerry's mother and our friends, but were rather shaken by the shabby, uncared-for condition of the zoo. In spite of a record season it was again up to its neck in a financial crisis and it was becoming increasingly obvious that the time had come to take over the reins ourselves. In order to take stock of the position, we commissioned our own accountants to do a financial survey of the administration and day-to-day running costs, and the result confirmed our worst fears. Quite apart from the financial side, several of our key staff were on the point of leaving.

As neither Gerry nor I were in a position to administer

the financial side of the zoo, it was vital to find someone who could come in and sort out the mess.

Half-heartedly, we put an advert in the local paper, which to our amazement produced a tremendous response. Some of the replies were quite impossible, but among them was one from Mrs. Weller. What we would have done without this ally who sorted out the administration, leaving us free to deal with animals, I cannot bear to think; we shall be for ever in her debt. Slowly but surely she introduced routine and order, and with the help of our many friends, things began to settle down. The kindness and support we received during this very anxious period was overwhelming.

Through the help of a friend, a group of influential people were persuaded to take an encouraging interest in the zoo's affairs, and Gerry decided that this was the moment to bring into being his long cherished dream of a Wildlife Preservation Trust. The zoo would become a public body, and in addition a scientific advisory board would be established. The aim of this Trust was to concentrate on keeping and breeding some of the countless numbers of creatures that were now being threatened with extermination in their natural state. It was a bold and ambitious proposal, but it was readily accepted by all the people now intimately concerned with the zoo's fate.

Expert advice was brought in and it was generally agreed that the first thing to do was to clear up the zoo's £15,000 of debts and start with a clean sheet. This is where the Jersey *Evening Post* proved of invaluable help. They published a letter composed and signed by twelve prominent people who were concerned with the zoo, and the response was overwhelming, donations ranging from £1,000 to a small boy's week's pocket money, and the donation that touched us the most was five guineas from the staff of Jersey Zoo.

Once again the people of Jersey showed their generosity. They had often supplied us with fruit, vegetables and meat free of charge in the past; now they soon had us well on the way to reaching our target. As our contribution to this effort, Gerry agreed to take full responsibility for the £20,000 loan and waive any right that he might have to recovering any of this from the zoo. By taking on the burden of this loan it means of course, since he relies entirely on his income from the books and from television, that he will be paying the money back for years to come. Many people said he was a fool, but Gerry felt passionately that this was one way in which he could help save some of the wildlife for future generations to enjoy.

Preparations for the coming season had to be put in hand and the I.C.I. kindly advised us on a new colour scheme to give the zoo a face-lift, and everyone worked till all hours making the place look neater and pleasanter for the public.

As if the worry about the zoo and its future were not enough, Gerry had to face another sad blow when his mother died suddenly, as the result of a heart attack. Everyone missed her, for she had been one of those rare people whom everyone loved, even if they had only met her quite casually. The house was a very sad place without her. One happy thing that happened during this period was that Sophie temporarily rejoined our ranks, which relieved the worry of a secretary for the moment. The Appeal and the Trust went swiftly forward and we also got notable additions to the zoo. The New Zealand Government gave us a pair of Tuataras and two pairs of Keas; Gerry bought a pair of young Orang Utangs; and we also exchanged some of the more common animals with a dealer and got a Spectacled Bear as part of the exchange. Pedro is the sweetest bear that any of us has ever met, and has become one of the main attractions of the zoo.

While we were battling with the zoo's problems, Chris had been busy on the television series, which was going to be called 'Two in The Bush'—Jim Saunders's suggestion. The film material was excellent; and in fact there was so much good stuff that Chris felt he could get seven programmes and not six out of it, using the kangaroo birth as the climax of the series. So as well as everything else, Durrell had now got to write a light-hearted commentary for it all, and spent hours closeted in his darkened office looking at the roughly cut film over and over again until we could not bear the sight of it. In a desperate attempt to help, Chris came over to Jersey.[1]

While he was with us we began to discuss another film idea. It had originally been suggested to us by Brother Larry when we had visited him near the Camargue, the Provençal home of the fighting bulls, the year before. The French themselves do not kill the local bulls but play with them. In many villages and towns in Provence there is an arena, sometimes an ancient Roman amphitheatre, sometimes a roughly constructed ring, where every weekend during the season enthusiasts gather to follow their favourite bulls with all the fervour of football fans. The object of the twelve or fifteen young men taking part is to remove the red cockades from between the bull's horns without getting gored in the process. The game lasts for twenty minutes and should a bull successfully outwit the contestants and keep all the cockades, *Carmen* is played in his honour as he is escorted from the ring by an ancient lead cow.

Larry was convinced it would make a wonderful documentary for television as it had everything a film-maker could desire : travel, colour, excitement, crowds of people, the bull-ring—but no gore. Durrell was thrilled with the idea and he had even worked out a rough script for Chris to show his department head. So during his brief visit Chris divided his time between the darkened office downstairs and our untidy flat upstairs, often staying up into the small hours to discuss the bull film.

At last the commentaries for 'Two in The Bush' were finished and we made a date to go over to Bristol for the recording session. By this time we were all beginning to feel a little apprehensive on Durrell's account, and were

[1] As Chris's idea of help is more hindrance than help, this did not help. G.D.

not in the least surprised when he developed a mysterious allergy and his arms started swelling up in the middle of recording.

Gerry's publishers were by now pressing him for another manuscript and he had made several attempts to write *Menagerie Manor*, but it is not easy to concentrate whole-heartedly on writing a carefree, happy book when one is beset on all sides by the problems arising from the very subject you are trying to be light-hearted about. If it had not been for Sophie and me he would have destroyed the lot, and never have I wished so fervently that I could write the book for him. By the time it was finished, none of us liked it very much, but we were in the minority for it was a great success. It was serialised in both the United Kingdom and in the States, various foreign publications published extracts, and the B.B.C. did it as 'A Book At Bedtime', as they had all his previous books.

'Two in The Bush' was a great success on television, which delighted us after all the hard work Jim and Chris had put into this series. Viewers were particularly impressed with the birth of the kangaroo, as we had hoped they would be.

It was encouraging to hear from Chris that the bull film might come off, though it rested on his going to the Camargue and seeing the area and the problems involved for himself. We were only too pleased to take him there, and as the zoo was by now working quite smoothly and had seemingly surmounted its difficulties, we felt that we could leave it safely for two or three weeks and go off with him.

We all piled into our tiny mini estate car and drove like mad things through the glorious French countryside to Nîmes, where Larry had installed us in a nice hotel. For the next fortnight we toured around the Camargue looking at bull-fights, looking at bulls in various stages of development, meeting all those people who might be able to help us, and generally setting things up for any future visit. By the end of our stay, Chris was wildly enthusiastic and was determined to do the film, if possible in colour, but it

was all a question of the budget. However, this could be
settled in Bristol when he got back. Even if nothing came
of it, we had at least had a slight break from the zoo and
all its worries, and when we eventually got back to Jersey,
we found that everyone had things running very smoothly.

'You know,' said Gerry, 'I think they all work far better
when I'm not here.'

This pleased me a great deal. 'Good, well perhaps we can
get away more often then and have some time to ourselves,'
I speculated. A grunt was the only reply I got.

A couple of weeks later, Chris told us triumphantly that
the bull film was to go ahead, even though the budget
would not go to colour film, and he came over again to
discuss Gerry's suggested story-line now that he had seen
the Camargue for himself. He thought it would need three
trips to the area : in the spring, summer and winter, and
although there was no need for us to go on the first two
trips, he felt he would like us there for the last one. I was
all for this; any excuse to eat French food and drink the
wine and get away from the zoo for a short time! When
you are confined on a small island and live in the middle of
a zoo at everyone's beck and call twenty-four hours a day,
one longs to get away. Even Durrell, who is devoted to
his animals, agrees with me. An occasional small break
also enables you to see your problems a little more
clearly and restore your balance, and if one can combine
the physical act of leaving with a perfectly justifiable
reason for doing so, then it eases the conscience.

While all this was going on, other things were getting
themselves organised. The Jersey Wildlife Preservation
Trust was finally a fact; monthly meetings of the Trustees
and Council were held, and two members of the Council
were co-opted on to the zoo management side, which
served to take a little of the responsibility and worry off
Gerry and Catha Weller. Yet despite this extra help,
Durrell seemed to be getting even more taken up with zoo
and Trust matters, and I seldom saw him alone or had
a conversation that was not interspersed with zoo problems.

I began to loathe the zoo or anything to do with it. The flat was becoming a second office, with a constant procession of people trailing up. I finally put my foot down and made Durrell promise to discuss zoo and Trust matters in his office downstairs, and leave us one small haven where we could try and relax and be on our own. But it was an uphill struggle and I often felt that I had married a zoo and not a human being.

In a small effort to keep part of our lives free, I resigned from the Trust Council and Zoo Management Committees, and was desperately looking round for something that might break the thread and get us away from Jersey, when Chris came to the rescue.

'Why don't we do another trip, Gerry, before the glow of "Two in The Bush" has gone off?'

'My dear boy, nothing would give me greater pleasure, but where can we go that either hasn't been done by others already or won't take too long to prepare? For instance, I'd love to go back to the Argentine, but that would take at least four months to organise. Guiana might be worthwhile, but there's still political unrest there at the moment and I had quite enough political trouble in Paraguay to want to risk getting involved in internal politics again. India would need careful preparation, so that only leaves West Africa really, and I have already written three books about that area, so I can't go back to the Cameroons. Where do you suggest?'

There was a small silence at the other end of the line.

'Well, you once mentioned Sierra Leone as a possibility.'

'Yes, but when do you want to go?'

'Not until February anyway, and I must be back by May to finish the bull film off.'

'You're not giving me much time, are you? Anyway, I'll go ahead and see what can be done.'

Durrell's attention was now completely focused on something other than the zoo, for which I was deeply grateful. Yet I knew that he loathed being rushed into things, especially ill-prepared expeditions, and that if he did decide to go on this trip, it would be with reluctance, for six weeks was no time at all to get things really under way. If it was to be Sierra Leone, then I was not going with them, and Durrell was not surprised when I said, 'No. I don't like West Africa, either the sticky heat or the tropical forests, for it all makes me feel claustrophobic and as you know I get exasperated by the Africans. So if you don't mind, I think I'll miss this one.'

Durrell said he had half expected this, but asked what I would do while he was away. 'You don't want to stay here, do you?'

I was equally firm about this, and it was decided that I should go out to the Argentine to do a recce for a possible trip to take place in the winter of 1966.

'I'll take the Land-Rover with me so that I can go round the country easily, and I'll contact all the officials that we met on our previous trip and let you know what things are like now compared to five years ago.'

I arranged to take two friends with me to act as co-drivers and interpreters. Mrs. Hope Platt wanted to go back to the Argentine almost as much as I did. She had spent many years there and spoke Spanish fluently. She was also a wonderful driver, and being a rather large lady was ideally suited to play the part of a formidable chaperon should the occasion arise. We had met my other companion, Ann Peters, on holiday in Corfu. She too was an excellent driver and having lived in Africa for some years was used to travelling over difficult terrain. The fact that Ann and I were very much younger than Mrs. Platt led to some hilarious complications for she was always taken for our mother; in sheer desperation we gave up trying to explain the relationship and from then on she was known to both of us as 'Mum'.

The thought of going back to the Argentine was wonderful. Before anyone could change their mind I contacted our bank and arranged to get on a cargo boat leaving roughly at the same time as Durrell. As I was not going to Sierra Leone I had no compunction in leaving all the organisation of the trip to Durrell and John Hartley whom Durrell was borrowing from the zoo's reptile house for the trip, with Sophie standing in the wings to rescue them if they got bogged down. They seemed to be coping very well indeed but I was living for the day when we all left and found it hard to concentrate on their plans. I nearly didn't get away, for the Argentine ship my party was booked on was held up on the Continent by strikes, but the Bank managed to find a British boat going at about the same time, and what was even nicer, it was cheaper. So I spent a couple of lazy days in London going to films and eating a great deal, and then had to tear across country to Newport to meet Durrell and Hartley on their way up to Liverpool. We were both a little solemn at the thought that we would not be together again for about four months, but I made Durrell promise that if anything happened and they found they needed extra help, they were to let me know immediately and I would come as quickly as I could; though I did underline that it must be a legitimate reason.

Both our ships suffered in severe January gales, and Durrell and I managed one hour together as our ships crossed at Las Palmas. He was nearly arrested by the Spanish authorities for dashing down the gangway, his arms laden with champagne bottles, for the ship had been cleared by Customs and Immigration. A large Spanish policeman grabbed him as he passed and forced him back on the ship. Fuming, he tried every ship's officer in an effort to get a release, while I stood on the quayside urging him on for our ship was due to leave. Eventually he found a sympathetic official, poured out the story of how he and I were going to be separated for months, and got his release. He sprinted over to our ship where our chief steward produced more champagne; for Durrell had been forced to leave his own on board.[2]

[2] The only occasion so far in my life where I have been arrested twice and drunk a magnum of warm champagne before 8.30 in the morning. G.D.

I sailed on in calmer seas towards South America to be met by an enthusiastic army of friends, and after only a week's wrangling with the Customs, I managed to extricate the Land-Rover and leave Buenos Aires.

As I had seen Patagonia before, I prevailed upon the other two to go towards the Andes. The country we passed through was magnificent, with flat-topped plateaus descending into valleys before climbing up again. The thing that distressed me a great deal was that we saw very little wildlife compared with all that we had seen on our previous two visits. I think there were two main reasons for this: the spread of communities, and the resulting spread of cultivation and the wide use of chemical sprays. However, while staying on one *estancia*, we did see quite a lot of wildfowl and other water birds, while the little guinea-pigs scurried across the roads and the odd oven bird shouted at us as we passed. But gone were the almost unbroken lines of burrowing owls perched on the fence posts; it was an event to see one.

The thing that appalled me about the entire trip was the bad weather. After all, I had come to South America to find sunshine, instead of which, certainly in the mountains, all we got was low-lying cloud, cold winds and a fine drizzle, and I had no real difficulty in persuading my companions to beat a retreat to warmer climes. Even Buenos Aires, which normally swelters in February, was relatively cool, for which I for one was thankful.

So we drove to Mendoza so that I could contact an Argentinian scientist whom Durrell had met before, about an elusive creature called the Fairy Armadillo. To capture one of these creatures had become almost an obsession with Durrell, and this scientist actually had some in his possession. Over the telephone he assured me that they were still there waiting for Durrell to come and take them, and he made me promise to pass this message on.

I then spent two days enjoying the city itself and the surrounding countryside and looking at the local zoo. As it was not autumn I did not see the glorious avenues of golden poplars that had met Durrell on his trip here in 1959, but nevertheless it was a well laid out, tree-lined city with beautiful parks and a good climate.

We were contemplating returning to Buenos Aires in a rather leisurely fashion, but Mrs. Platt received an urgent cable summoning her back, and so we had to tear ourselves away and dash across the country to Buenos Aires where she could catch a plane. I intended to linger a little longer in the Republic, but to get a return passage on a cargo boat is not easy, and I thought it better to take the Dutch ship that was offered, even though it meant transhipping at Rotterdam.

During the whole of the time that I had been in the Argentine, I had not received a word from Sierra Leone. This did not worry me unduly, but I was anxious to be back in the United Kingdom to meet the Sierra Leone collection in May. So we sailed from Buenos Aires, making several long and unscheduled stops along the Brazilian coast, which was very pleasant, especially when we heard that Northern Europe was, as usual, in the grip of a cool spell.

During our voyage, I exchanged quite a flourish of cables with Catha Weller in Jersey, including one from Gerry asking me to meet him in Freetown. Then began a long, involved cable exchange with the bank in London in an effort to get me on a ship that would reach Freetown before they all sailed on 1st May. There was only one ship that would get me there in time, but would I be back in England in time to catch it? At our present rate of progress it seemed that the answer was no. However, to everyone's surprise, I think including the captain's, we docked at Rotterdam on 5th April, which left me approximately twenty-four hours to get back to London, arrange for the return of the Land-Rover, gather my wits and dash up to Liverpool to catch the *Accra*. It is an experience that I would not like to repeat, for after five weeks on a Dutch cargo boat I was looking forward to a brief stay on dry land.

The journey out to Freetown was quite amusing and everyone went out of their way to make me feel at home. Durrell and company had travelled out on this boat and would be returning on it. The whole ship was looking forward to carrying the collection of animals, and no one seemed to believe that I honestly did not know what had been caught.

It was strange to be in Las Palmas again within five days, but we did not stay long. I was told that we would dock in Freetown at around six o'clock in the morning and so there I was standing forrard watching Freetown loom into view through the early morning mist, assuming that in view of my mad dash to join him, my spouse would at least be there to greet me. I was doomed to disappointment. Everyone else's friends, relatives and what-have-you seemed to be there, but of Durrell there was no sign. The ship's agent finally rooted me out and told me that my husband was trying unsuccessfully to get on to the quayside. As usual, Durrell had forgotten that he needed a permit and was battling with police and dock officials.

'Come on, let's go and rescue him,' said the agent, and together we went down on to the quayside and towards the Customs building. Sure enough, there on a veranda above me stood a rather weary-looking Durrell hiding under a thicker undergrowth of beard than was normal, waving madly and complaining bitterly that he could not get down. Eventually the misunderstanding was settled and he was actually standing before me. He warned me not to be too boisterous with him for he thought he had broken a rib, and introduced me to a rather strange, gangling young man following in his wake, who turned out to be an American Peace Corps member who had kindly driven him down from up-country to meet me. Before I could say anything else Durrell thrust a small cardboard box into my hands.

'It's alive, so be careful how you open it,' he warned. Very gingerly, for I knew that Durrell would conceal the most obnoxious creatures in boxes, I opened the lid, and there nestling in a mound of tissues was a tiny little squirrel, rather like Small. It was an enchanting little thing and very tame.

'It was born to one of the squirrels in our collection and I thought that it was an ideal opportunity to get you a replacement for Small.'

No doubt many women would have been appalled to have been presented with a squirrel to mark a reunion, but I am used to receiving animals as gifts on notable occasions and had once asked to be given a pair of the beautiful Crown Pigeons as an anniversary present. At least it prevents me from having a stockpile of unwanted bottles of perfume and other useless gifts.

'Where's everybody else?' I asked.

'Oh, they're still up-country. They're coming down tomorrow with the entire collection. I brought a few of the delicate things down with me and they're at the British High Commission.'

He was obviously very pleased to see me and I think secretly a little relieved. His rib was very painful, but he had very stupidly forgotten that he had some pain-killing drugs in the medical kit that our doctor had supplied him with. I found these at the bottom of the chest and they appeared to give him some relief. He had broken the rib in the back of the Land-Rover. Chris, in his eagerness to get on with the job, had started the vehicle up before Durrell had sat down and Gerry had lost his balance and thumped himself on the tail-board. I discovered that he had been suffering with this rib since March, but he absolutely refused to leave everything and fly home with me.

It soon became obvious that we would need even more help, for if Gerry was to take the collection home by sea and finish the filming on board, he would need as much rest as possible. Young John Hartley had never taken a collection of animals back by sea before, and as he too appeared in the film series I decided that the actual looking after of the main collection should be my responsibility.

In order to have a second hand, as it were, I cabled Ann Peters who had been with me on the Argentine trip. She duly appeared in twenty-four hours, having caught the first plane, and when the collection had reached Freetown and been settled in at the luxurious Diamond Corporation flats where we were all staying, I could take stock of the situation.

Although we could relieve Durrell of the actual animal feeding routine, we could not go to visit the various Ministers and arrange for Customs permits and so on. This he would have to do himself. Still, we evolved a fairly simple routine. The shopping which had to be done daily for animal food was done by our American friend and John Hartley. Chris and Durrell were then free to visit Ministers and officials, and attend to urgent correspondence, while Ann and I coped with the animals, that is, all except such big things as the leopards which were left to the two boys. It worked extremely well, and in the fortnight before we actually left Freetown, we managed to get the animals fairly well established.

Transporting our equipment and animals down to the quayside was a problem, but here the Sierra Leone Army came to our help through one of their officers, Major Genda, whom Gerry had befriended when he first got to Freetown. He promised that three army vehicles would be put at our disposal, and sure enough at six o'clock on the morning of 1st May three large army Bedfords appeared.

A charming Customs man attended to us personally on the quayside, and in a very short time the animals, our two Land-Rovers and we ourselves were all installed on board the ship. The area allocated to us was right up forrard in a covered area referred to as Krootown, and it was ideal, being a semi-hold. If we had any bad weather, we could keep the animals fairly warm and comfortable, and in warm weather the hatch covers could be left off quite safely. There were also large shutters in the side of the ship itself that could be lifted up.

It took us a couple of days to get ourselves properly organised. Fortunately there was a kitchen with a hot water boiler nearby, and we were allowed full use of this. Even Chris used to give us a hand with the feeding, once he had got over the first day of feeling seasick. Although the weather was not rough, the ship was rather top heavy and rolled in the slightest swell. In the bows the motion was increased. The two leopards were exercised by John and Gerry, while the cleaning out was left to Ann and me. This also happened with the three young chimpanzees that we had, and with a very small red river hog. The rest of the animals could easily be cleaned out while they were still in their cages.

As the return voyage with a collection of animals had never been shown on television before, Chris was eager to show how the normal life of a passenger ship continued in spite of having an animal collection on board. The chief steward, Mr. Ryan, introduced us to the baker and the butcher and showed us where all the food that had been shipped out from England for us was stored. Every morning a certain amount of this would be delivered by the African stewards. The ship's carpenter was also an invaluable ally and when it was thought that the weather might get rough, he made a structure to support the cages on the deck.

Because of the number of children on board, we had asked the master and the purser if everyone could be told to keep well away, just in case someone was bitten. After one or two stray people had been carefully escorted from our part of the ship, the passengers did, on the whole, behave very well. During the fine weather the three chimpanzees were taken up on deck to sun themselves and play on the hatch cover. Naturally they were a tremendous attraction and it looked as if all the passengers on the ship were watching them from the upper deck. As the winds became stronger and cooler, though, we had to confine their daily exercise to the lower deck, which pleased Jimmy, one of the chimps, as he strongly objected to the wind whistling in his rather large ears.

The Master took a great liking to Jimmy and invited him up on to the bridge where he was immediately at home, even climbing on to a special stool to help steer the ship in a very professional manner. He and we were then entertained in the Captain's quarters and I think Jimmy was sorry to leave.

Our stewardess could not have been sweeter. Often in mid-morning or mid-afternoon she would appear with a large Thermos of tea or coffee, or if we happened to be in our cabins, would readily make us hot drinks or produce even stronger drinks if she felt we needed them. The laundry too was a tremendous help to us, for it is very easy to get dirty trying to cope with an animal collection on a heaving ship.

When we docked at Las Palmas to take on oil, we all scattered over the town in search of fresh fruit and greens to tempt the Colobus Monkeys. We had seven of these very rare, delicate, leaf-eating monkeys, and it was entirely due to the efforts of Ann Peters that these creatures survived the journey, and indeed still survive, for she laid the whole basis of their diet. It was almost as if she willed them to live, and she would spend hours in front of each cage hand-feeding them piece by piece. So it was with reluctance that she left us in Liverpool to go back to London by train while we were to fly by special charter flight direct to Jersey. The idea behind this plan was very sound. Not only would it enable Chris and his team to finish the filming in a relatively short time, but, we thought, it would be the easiest and least nerve-racking method of getting the animals to Jersey. But we reckoned without the plane.

The day started extremely well and for a May day in England the weather was good. The Customs clearing our baggage were very efficient and soon all the animals were being unloaded on to the dockside, and placed in the two large furniture vans we had hired to take us to the airport. It was at this juncture that officialdom took over and we became entangled with yards of red tape that threatened to strangle us all. The first thing was that somehow all the documents relating to the Land-Rovers had gone astray, and the poor R.A.C. man was faced with a dilemma. The vehicles were the property of the Rover Company who had kindly loaned them for use on the expedition, but we ourselves had no proof of this. Anyway, eventually it was decided that these vehicles be placed in bond and the Rover Company asked to clear them. We felt very guilty about this, but as it was not our fault that the documents had gone astray, we could do nothing but hope that Rovers would forgive and understand.

The second lot of documents that had not appeared were the Ministry of Agriculture permits, permitting the importation of the animals and in particular of the two leopards. Because of the quarantine regulations covering the importation of dogs and cats, a special dispensation had to be got from the English Ministry permitting us to land and take in transit the two leopards. Catha Weller in conjunction with Chris's secretary in Bristol had been in touch with the Ministry and had got their agreement to allow the leopards to land, but the permits had not arrived.

After hours of arguing with the official on duty, he agreed to contact the Ministry direct, and it eventually turned out that through some clerical error the licences had been sent to Jersey instead of to Liverpool. At any other time this would have been amusing, but we had all been up since dawn and were by that time feeling hungry and very tired. Apart from this, our animals had been confined in the furniture vans and some of them needed to be fed again, and we were also worried that we would be late for the plane. We were not sorry to leave Liverpool docks.

On our arrival at Speke Airport, we found to our relief that the plane had not come, and so we all went to have a quick drink before tackling the problem of unloading the animals and weighing them one by one on the airline's machine. This had to be done because in an air-freighter the weight has to be carefully dispersed throughout the whole body of the plane, but it was a nerve-racking procedure both for the animals and for us. We were just getting ready to load up the Bristol Freighter when the pilot announced that he was not satisfied with the performance of the port engine. Naturally we were relieved at his concern for our safety, but our relief soon turned to dismay when we learned that the only certified engineer who could touch the engine was in Manchester and we would have to wait several hours until he could be brought to Liverpool. There were lots of engineers on duty at the airport, but none of them had a licence to repair this particular plane.

We unloaded the animals into one of the hangars, away from the main airport noise, and began an interminable wait until the engineer finally appeared and at around half past eight pronounced the aircraft fit to take off. The animals and we were quickly loaded into the freighter, the doors closed, we fastened our safety belts, waved goodbye to the few people who had helped us, and the plane moved to the end of the runway. The pilot began to warm up the engines and when he had reached maximum revs the other engine began to back-fire. We were not surprised when we trundled to the end of the runway and turned back again. Fortunately, our helpers had not disappeared, nor had the engineer who examined the engine and said he could do nothing until he could get some spares the following morning.

We held a hurried conference with the airline's officials and decided to unload the really delicate animals and put them in a small room at the end of one of the hangars and cover them with tarpaulins. The rest we felt could stay in the plane overnight without any harm coming to them. The airline then fixed us all up in a hotel while we hurriedly fed the animals that we had unloaded, and at around eleven-thirty, absolutely dead on our feet, staggered to our hotel and, after a hot bath, went to bed.[3]

It must have been about two o'clock in the morning when we were awakened by the hotel manager. Apparently there was a large policeman standing on the doorstep, a little concerned because one of our animals was said to

[3] It's quicker by air. G.D.

be on the rampage inside the plane. Poor Durrell dragged himself out of bed, dressed hurriedly, and went downstairs. However, he reappeared within a few minutes. It turned out that an airport policeman on normal patrol had heard peculiar noises coming from the inside of a plane, and not knowing what it was, had been naturally concerned. No one had thought to tell this poor little man that there was a consignment of animals in the freighter. However, Gerry insisted on investigating, only to find that it was the leopards snuffling in their crates, and there was nothing to worry about.

We had arranged to meet the owner of the two furniture vans that had transported us from the docks at the airport at about 7 o'clock the following morning, and he had very kindly undertaken to get us some fresh lettuce and fruit. Sure enough, there he was when we got there, and he even helped us to clean and feed the chimps and the Colobus. We were all anxious to know how long we would have to wait for the aeroplane to be repaired, but no one seemed to know. None of the airline people, including the pilot, could have been nicer or more helpful, but this did nothing to relieve our anxiety about the plight of the animals still in the plane.

When it became obvious by mid-morning that the plane was still not fit to take off, we decided to unload the rest of the animals and feed them, and we began to badger the airline's head offices in London to provide another plane. Just when we were all beginning to despair and think that we would never get away, another air-freight line offered to send up one of their spare freighters. How Durrell stood the strain of coping with his rib, his tiredness and the worry of the animals, I shall honestly never know, but I felt that he was pretty near collapse. Then another problem presented itself; there were only two seats on the plane that was coming up to take the animals, and there were six of us. It was essential that the camera man and the sound recordist get to Jersey in order to take film of the arrival of the animals at the zoo, and here Cambrian Airways came to our help and offered us four spare seats on their Jersey flight. After a long argument, Durrell and Hartley stayed behind with the animals, while Chris and I flew on to Jersey with his crew.

At the airport in Jersey everyone was waiting for us. The entire zoo staff was arrayed on the runway, together with the Land-Rover, the zoo van, and three trucks, and we anxiously scanned the skies hoping that the sea mist for which Jersey is famous would not drift in before the aircraft touched down. We need not have worried because dead on time the large DC4 made its landing approach and came to rest exactly opposite where we were all standing.

The Jersey Customs could not have been more helpful, and, although they did not know about our wrangles with their English counterparts the previous day, it was almost as though they were trying to compensate for their obstructiveness. I could tell that Gerry was thankful to hand his animals over to the staff, and soon they were all released into their new quarters, most of them completely unaffected by the strain and the stress of the long delay. As usual, it appeared to be the poor human beings who had suffered the most.

The next morning, Gerry and Chris went round the zoo. Everyone was dashing around seeing that our charges were well looked after and getting the titbits that they were used to, and I warned them all about the Colobus.

'If anything happens to them, be ready to face an irate Miss Peters when she gets here next week. She's nurtured these things all the way from Freetown. So for God's sake don't let anything happen to them now they have arrived.'

The leopards were quite unperturbed and were happily playing with John. The squirrels and mongooses also settled well in their new quarters and the birds, particularly the owls, were concerned with only one thing—eating as much as possible as quickly as possible. Durrell was happy, as indeed we all were, and he could now collapse—at least for another twenty-four hours.

Chris and his crew departed the next day and we planned

to go away as soon as we could get everything settled and the Durrell rib was whole once more. But I should have known better. The zoo and its affairs encroached further and further into our lives and we are still here. And I know only too well that wherever we go there will always be animals and that my bed will never be free.[4]

[4] Certainly not while I'm alive. G.D.

Fontana Books

Fontana is best known as one of the leading paperback publishers of popular fiction and non-fiction. It also includes an outstanding, and expanding section of books on history, natural history, religion and social sciences.

Most of the fiction authors need no introduction. They include Agatha Christie, Hammond Innes, Alistair MacLean, Catherine Gaskin, Victoria Holt and Lucy Walker. Desmond Bagley and Maureen Peters are among the relative newcomers.

The non-fiction list features a superb collection of animal books by such favourites as Gerald Durrell and Joy Adamson.

All Fontana books are available at your bookshop or newsagent; or can be ordered direct. Just fill in the form below and list the titles you want.

FONTANA BOOKS, Cash Sales Department, P.O. Box 4, Godalming, Surrey. Please send purchase price plus 5p postage per book by cheque, postal or money order. No currency.

NAME (Block letters)

ADDRESS